DREAMBOATS

Hollywood Hunks of the '50s

Other books by Maria Ciaccia:

Bloomin', A Novel in Three Acts

Complete Preparation: A Guide to Auditioning for Opera (Joan Dornemann with Maria Ciaccia)

Hollywood Hunks DREAMBOATS of the '50s

by Maria Ciaccia

Excalibur Publishing
New York

Published by:
Excalibur Publishing
434 Avenue of the Americas, Suite 790
New York, New York 10011

Cover and graphic design: Kara Glasgold, Griffin Design

Library of Congress Cataloging in Publication Data

Ciaccia, Maria.
    Dreamboats : Hollywood hunks of the '50s / by Maria Ciaccia.
        p.   cm.
    ISBN 0-9627226-4-2 (pbk.)
    1. Motion picture actors and actresses--Biography. 2. Motion
picture actors and actresses--Portraits.   I. Title.
PN1998.2.C564   1992
791.43'028'0922--dc20
    [B]   92-19150

Printed in Mexico

1 2 3 4 5 6 7 8 9 10

This book is dedicated to

BARRY PARIS

who wouldn't let me lose my dream,
and then helped it come true

Table of Contents

Acknowledgments

There would have been no book without the support of my parents, Alfred and Cecilia Ciaccia, in this project.

The graciousness and generosity of the following people have contributed immeasurably to *Dreamboats*: Tony Curtis, Farley Granger and John Ericson, dreamboats inside as well as out; Rita Gam, who not only spoke with me, but told me I could quote whatever was relevant from her two books; Jack Larson, who gave me so much of his time and insight; Meyer Mishkin, refreshing and wonderful; and my dear friend Lee Riordan. Tony Randall went out of his way to speak with me, and I will never forget his kindness.

The beautiful photographs in this book are a result of the research done by the Kobal Collection, particularly Bob Cosenza, who was very generous with his time, and by Howard Mandelbaum, Ron Mandelbaum and Henry Fera at Photofest. My afternoons at Photofest were joyous, with Howard, Ron and Henry's wonderful anecdotes and suggestions. Thanks also to the Billy Rose Collection of the New York Public Library, and the Margaret Herrick Library of the Academy of Motion Picture Arts and Sciences.

On the home front, Beth Allen, publicist major domo extraordinaire, proved again her amazing gifts with people, and Sharon Good's encouragement and technical advice was a constant. I would also like to acknowledge the support of Howard Cutler, Celeste Ciaccia, David Stenn, Ellen Martin, Trish Caroselli Rintels, Kathleen Fogarty, Skip E. Lowe, Richard Lamparski, George Smith, Bill Cappello, David Hamblin, Stan Bartosiak, Kara Glasgold, and my new friend, Zachary Morgan.

DREAMBOATS

Hollywood Hunks of the '50s

Robert Wagner and Jeffrey Hunter, 20th Century Fox juvenile stars.

Such Stuff As
Dreams Are Made On

Dreamboats: Hollywood Hunks of the '50s has been a project of mine for the last six years. During that time, the '50s has been in and out of fashion, but one thing has remained: our love of nostalgia. The future is so scary that the past seems more attractive and comforting, a reminder of what seems like a safer, happier time. Alas, it is only safer and happier in retrospect. As Jack Larson told me during our interview, "History is a lie, you know." He's right.

The men in this book project dazzling images of youth from another era. Today, in our society, youth is becoming a more precious commodity than ever, as the population ages and we watch some of our young die from drugs and AIDS. But youth died in the '50s, too, in war, from polio and from many of the maladies that plague our world today.

The '50s were no less confusing than the '90s. Looking at these photographs, one will notice the mixed messages of the good, clean, all-American boys and those dangerous, hoodlum types, with their threatening sexuality. Post-war, there were dark undercurrents that couldn't help but surface. As returning soldiers and their families went after the American dream, young people found society impossible to relate to, with its images of death and threat of atomic war. Alienated from their parents, they began to question the religious and moral

A class for young hopefuls at Universal Studios. Center: Drama teacher Sophie Rosenstein. Note Tony Curtis at lower left and Rock Hudson at upper right.

values imposed on them. Living wild in the streets became the order of the day.

As a reflection of this upheaval, the film industry changed drastically post-war, along with the rest of society. The inner workings of the movie business went through a metamorphosis, and so did the films. With all the returning war hero stories, war stories and war hero psychological re-adjustment stories, the women's pictures that had been such a big part of the '40s — and the women stars — began to take a back seat. Actresses such as Barbara Stanwyck and Loretta Young were reduced to playing housewives. There were more male stars and more male-oriented movies. To this day, women still have not reclaimed the film dominance they enjoyed in the '30s and '40s, although the trend seems to be shifting again.

As the '50s progressed, the studios came grinding to a halt. Anti-trust laws finally compelled the motion picture companies to divest themselves of their theater chains, the government decreeing that studio control over what was shown in theaters constituted a monopoly. This decision opened competition to independent producers. The stranglehold the studios had on what was produced and shown in theaters was over. This, added to the growing popularity of television, meant major problems in Hollywood.

Tony Randall was there when the studios were in collapse. "I came in — I was a contract player at Twentieth Century Fox at the very end of that era. By the time I came, television had done its damage to the studio system. The studios no longer had the great lists of players. The mighty sound stages were mostly standing vacant. I remember wandering onto a sound stage, and there in a corner were four men singing a Pepsi-Cola commercial. So by the late '50s, the studios were already renting out those enormous sound stages to anyone who would use them for a day. The great era was over."

But before these threats and problems, when the war ended, it was back to business as usual. The male stars were older now, and wartime replacements such as Turhan Bey and Paul Henried had not really filled their shoes. It was time for some new blood. The studio criteria were the same as they had always been: looks, presence, potential or, in rare cases, obvious acting ability. Talent scouts invaded the college campuses and the New York stage. In these places, they found many of the men and boys in this book.

Jack Larson, friend of Montgomery Clift, in his days as Jimmy Olsen on *Superman*. Photo credit: William Claxton

As with the female stars, "classic" looks — even features, beautiful physiques and a predilection for dark hair and blue eyes — were the order of the day. A young actor attempting success in the '50s told me, "Everybody had to look like Rock Hudson, and if they didn't, they couldn't get work." Lee Marvin said, "I was never under contract to any one studio. People like Tab Hunter were being signed. But not character actors."

Tab Hunter was unusual in that he was blond in a sea of dark hair. Blond leading men have always been a rarity. And unheard of in the '50s were minorities as "hunks." Their sad lack is evident throughout this book. Sal Mineo stood alone in the pre-*Godfather* era as an ethnic presence. And there was certainly no such thing as multi-racial casting in the '50s. I asked Rita Gam, who played Egyptians, Indians and gypsies, to comment on this: "There was a running gag — who's got the darker pancake. They'd take these perfectly wonderful heroes and heroines who should have been black, who should have been Chinese, who should have been American Indian, who should have been Indian, and they took the closest thing they could find." Witness Jeff Chandler as Cochise in *Broken Arrow*, Jeffrey Hunter as an Indian in *White Feather*, and Marlon Brando in *Teahouse of the August Moon*. Jeff Chandler was once

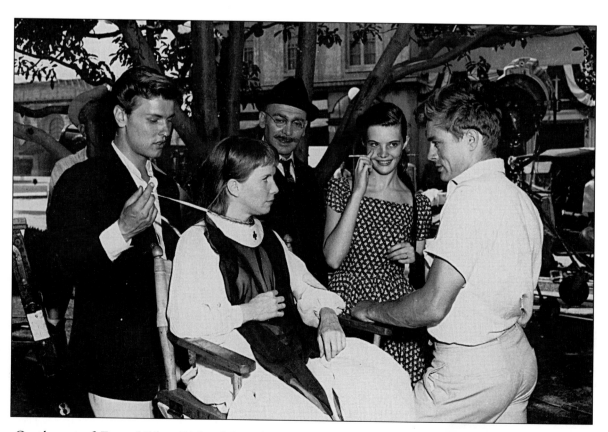

On the set of *East of Eden*: Richard Davalos, Julie Harris, James Dean. Warner Brothers, 1955.

Lucky Lady: Jeanne Crain hangs out at the Jug Room with Jeffrey Hunter and Dale Robertson in *Take Care of My Little Girl*. 20th Century Fox, 1951.

described as a "one-man United Nations," playing Israelis, Irishmen, Indians, Hawaiians and Poles.

For those who complain that films and theater haven't progressed far enough in the way of multi-racial casting, I would agree. But today's celebrities do reflect the American "melting pot" in a way that the '50s and before never did, as this book testifies.

Name changing was another attempt at homogenization. Studios always changed names they felt to be difficult or not glamorous enough. In the postwar era, stars either had similar names, like Jeffrey Hunter (Henry McKinnies, Jr.) and Jeff Chandler (Ira Grossel), for instance, or quirky names like Rock Hudson (Roy Scherer) and Tab Hunter (Art Gelien). Rita Gam, who has one of these catchy Hollywood names (although in her case, it is her real name), said, "The name lives by itself. If you have one of these quotable names, you always have a life in the newspapers." Due to the ethnicity of his appearance, and a previous Broadway career, Sal Mineo was allowed to keep his name. One wonders what names Travolta, Pacino, Hoffmann, de Niro or Stallone might have had under the studio system (or if some of them would have been made stars at all).

Jeff Chandler and Rock Hudson during the filming of *Iron Man*. Universal, 1951.

Rita Gam and Jeff Chandler in *Sign of the Pagan*. Universal, 1954.

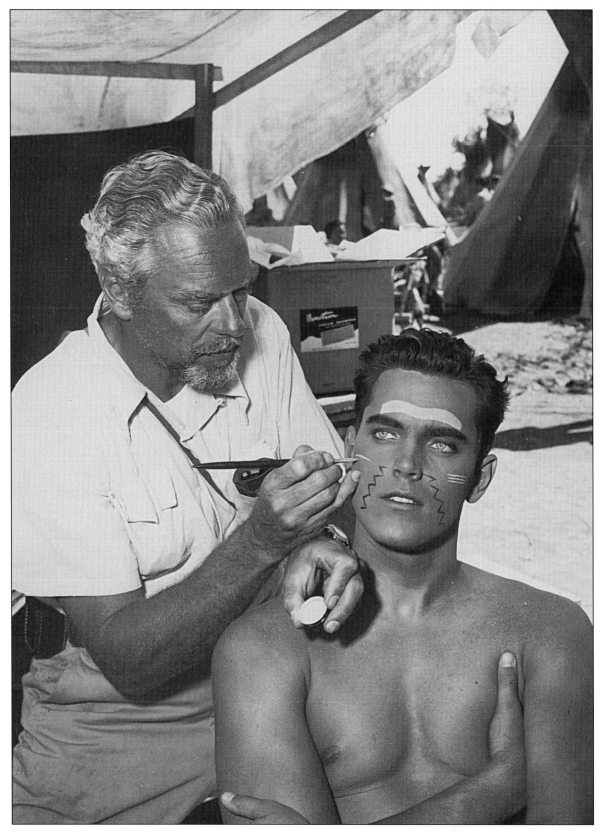

Jeffrey Hunter gets into Indian make-up for *White Feather*. 20th Century Fox, 1955.

What was it like to be under contract in the'50s? What was Hollywood like? What was the social life like, depending on your status? I asked three people — Rita Gam, who had a star contract at MGM; director-turned-writer Lee Riordan, a contract player at Twentieth Century Fox in the early '50s after a screen test arranged by his friend Jeffrey Hunter; and talent scout, then casting director, then agent Meyer Mishkin.

Rita Gam: "There was a sterility about Hollywood that is very hard to explain. The mores and expectations were as bound as a book of etiquette. There were things that you did and things that you didn't do. The caste system was so total and so complete. The tone of a voice was prescribed by the size of your contract. And knowing that was, in a way, reassuring, because you knew where you stood all the time. You were protected by it. You were lonely. A lot of stars never come back from that trip.

"Everyone smiles in California. The smile of the guard at the studio always projected how 'in' you were. They gave a bigger smile to a big star. The make-up people were very sweet, and the hairdressers were very sweet — everyone was very sweet, but underneath there was this terror of the front office. There was the terror of Louella Parsons and Hedda Hopper. They were taken very seriously. There was a great deal of terror in California."

Lee Riordan: "The word was that my screen test had gone well, although they thought my ears were a bit big. I had a standard contract at Fox. There were an awful lot of people under contract. This was the era when just about anyone fairly good-looking was able to get a 'seven-year, we can drop the option at any time' contract. I attended a few classes with other young people in my category, people who would play supporting roles. Most of them had not had much, if any, training as actors. Debra Paget was in my group. These acting classes were pretty disorganized, held at the students' convenience, when they could get a group together. They were usually in the evening. The classes were mandatory, but set up where they'd say, 'We're going to have ten classes, and you have to go to at least four of them.'

"I was in *Fourteen Hours*, and I played a fraternity snob in *Take Care of My Little Girl* — Dale Robertson starred and Jeffrey Hunter had one of his early roles in it. I was invited to Darryl Zanuck's parties, where I had two conversations with Marilyn Monroe.

"Hank [Jeffrey Hunter] and I double-dated a lot. A place that we liked particularly to take our dates was the dinner spot in the Hollywood Roosevelt Hotel. It had a Hawaiian theme. Waiters wore Hawaiian shirts, and at a certain point in the evening, as guests sat eating, flashes of lightening would occur over

Two dramatic poses: Farley Granger and Ruth Roman in *Strangers on a Train* . . .
Warner Brothers, 1951.

. . . and Jeff Chandler and Joan Crawford in *Female on the Beach*. Universal, 1955.

14

Dale Robertson and Anne Francis do a publicity pose for *Lydia Bailey.*
20th Century Fox, 1952.

the bar. The waiters would announce a storm was approaching and raise the umbrellas over each table, as a deluge of water came down from the ceiling. The waiters stood in the downpour, as if it were the monsoons. They'd just leave all the water on the floor. In another hour or so, there'd be another storm. Once the waiters got wet, they were just wet for the rest of the evening, I guess." Just a typical Hollywood night on the town.

Agent Meyer Mishkin, who at different times in his long career has handled such celebrities as Jeff Chandler, Lee Marvin, Jack Palance, Richard Dreyfuss, Lindsay Wagner, Richard Crenna and Mare Winningham, commented about the old Hollywood. "I'd meet Jeff Chandler for lunch at Universal, and I would sit there with Jeff, Tony Curtis, Piper Laurie — they were all the young people who were working for Universal under contract. They had another actor who was not even being used very well named Rock Hudson. All of them were tied up in those seven-year deals. Did Tony Curtis tell you what his contract was for? Seventy-five dollars a week. He worked twenty out of twenty-six weeks. It was a very difficult time, except that, remember in those days, if you were able to put an actor under contract to a studio, at least he had a steady place to go.

"When I was a talent scout for Fox, what I was up against was the fact that we were always looking for leading men and leading women. I, in turn, when I covered theaters in summer stock and in communities, would make my own notes about the people I felt were talented. I didn't care how they looked. I watched them work, and I would sometimes see them in a succession of plays and saw them developing their talents, learning how to handle themselves."

The studios had to choose, and when I sat down to write *Dreamboats: Hollywood Hunks of the '50s,* I found myself in a similar position. In selecting "hunks," I could not possibly include every matinee idol from the '50s, so I chose to eliminate people whose careers were based mainly in television, such as Robert Horton. I also eliminated carryovers from the '40s — Robert Mitchum, Burt Lancaster and William Holden, et al — concentrating instead on those who appealed to the teens, the readers of the "fan mags." Also left out were recording stars, although many of them appeared in films.

A word about Elvis, that ultimate '50s icon. With so much written about him and so many photographs published, and the fact that in the '50s, he was predominantly a rock 'n' roll star, I decided to leave space for those who have

Rock Hudson and Tony Randall in *Send Me No Flowers.* Universal, 1964.

James Dean and director Nicholas Ray during the filming of *Rebel Without A Cause*.
Warner Brothers, 1955.

been less well-covered in the past. Also, as far as Elvis' film career is concerned, the bulk of his work was done in the '60s. Before going into the Army in the late '50s, he made only four films.

With so many of the celebrities deceased, obtaining interviews for this book was a challenge, to say the least, a challenge helped along by the people I met along the way. The day after I interviewed Tony Curtis, I was sitting at my desk frantically transcribing the rather hard-to-hear tape I had recorded of my interview with him, when my phone rang.

"Hello."

"Is Maria there?" Well, I had just been listening to Tony Curtis on tape, and darned if this didn't sound like him on the phone!

"This is Maria."

"Tony Curtis. Did I wake you?"

"No, Mr. Curtis, I was just listening to your interview."

"Well, we mustn't forget John Derek." (See the chapter on Derek for Tony's comments.)

"He's in the book, Mr. Curtis."

"Well, I just wanted to say 'hello'."

Then there was the fabulous, beautiful Rita Gam, always working on a hundred projects, including her autobiography, *Nine Lives*. She answered her phone, breathless. I reminded her who I was, and we exchanged greetings.

"Rita — is this a good time to talk?"

"Oh, yes."

"Can you talk to me about working with Jeff Chandler?"

"I certainly can. But I can't do it now."

Trying to find Tab Hunter, Dale Robertson and Rory Calhoun would make a book in itself. Having long since realized that agents and managers weren't the way to go, I took an indirect route. Needless to say, leaving messages in a restaurant for a friend of Tab Hunter's in Virginia didn't work, and although I tracked down Dale Robertson to an obscure location, he still hasn't answered my letter. The worst of all was hearing from several people that Rory Calhoun was dead, and having his agent tell me he didn't know if he was dead or alive. Calling the Screen Actors Guild was another experience — when I had to spell Tab Hunter's name, I seriously questioned if I should do the book or not.

Most of the men pictured on these pages are there because of their physical

Out on the town: Rock Hudson with Joyce Holden and Marilyn Maxwell.

Tony Curtis with Janet Leigh.

Tab Hunter and fans, 1954.

appearance, that's true. But was every '50s dreamboat just "a pretty face with naught behind it?" No. But in some cases, the "pretty face" was the entire reason for a beginning success, and when the star didn't deliver anything else, he found his success fleeting. Most of these gentlemen were lucky, at least in the beginning of their careers, to have the movie studios handling and guiding them. The demise of the studios left these and future budding stars to their own devices.

Today's young performers have no studios and no grooming. Meyer Mishkin said, "What I feel nowadays is that some of the actors are becoming stars too quickly. In those days, at least they were given opportunities to learn the entertainment business. Now, they accidentally, we'll say, get into a film, and the picture accidentally does well at the box office. And immediately somebody casts them in another film, in a picture that is not a good one, and they want to know why the young actor isn't able to carry it. Hardly any grooming nowadays." Tony Randall puts it this way: "Nobody builds you today. No matter what kind of hit you make in a movie, you have to still go out and look for your next job."

A young actor or actress in the '90s, to overcome some of these mine fields, not only has to have talent and discipline, but a good business sense, excellent taste in scripts, strong career goals, and an ability to surround him or herself with the right people. And even with all that, their fame may be fleeting. And of all fame, none is more fleeting than teen-idol status. Moving on from there is a massive undertaking.

The way of a '50s hunk was predictable. For a time, each hunk's photo adorned the walls of teenage girls growing up in the '50s. For a time, his studio received huge amounts of fan mail for him. For a time, there were huge stories written about him in fan magazines. For a time, he was part of big-budget films. For a time . . . until his time passed, as unfortunately, with "hunks," it always does. But as evidenced by their photos, the stars on these pages all deserved to shine brightly, and did. Hundreds and hundreds of young people were brought to Hollywood in the '50s, and very few made the grade with the studios. As Tony Curtis said, "We were the elite. We were under contract."

Maria Ciaccia
New York City, 1992

Marlon Brando
A Truant Disposition

Marlon Brando has an angel in his soul, and it has never left him. When he is so inclined nowadays, he can still dazzle audiences, although, unfortunately, he doesn't work as often as he once did. Laurence Olivier, when told he had influenced more young actors than anyone else, disagreed. He believed that honor belonged to Brando. He was right.

Discipline, however, has never been Brando's strong suit. Perhaps his unsettled childhood contributed to that failing. He was born on April 3, 1924, in Omaha, Nebraska, but in short order, because of Marlon Brando, Sr.'s work as a salesman, the family moved to Evanston, Illinois, Santa Ana, California and Libertyville, Illinois. Brando's love for the theater came from his mother, whom he adored. (She co-starred with Henry Fonda in *Beyond the Horizon* at the Omaha Community Playhouse.) However, Brando's early ambition, he told Sidney Skolsky in 1955, "was to be a drummer."

He displayed a vivid imagination and a talent for mimicry as a young student, but considered uncontrollable, his father enrolled him in a military academy. Brando raged against the school's precise order and rules and was ultimately expelled, but not before he smashed his knee playing football, an injury which eliminated him from the Army.

On the set of *A Streetcar Named Desire*: Kim Hunter, Karl Malden and Marlon Brando.
Warner Brothers, 1951.

After several dead-end jobs, Brando at 19 headed for New York, gravitating
after a time to the New School for Social Research, where he and his sister,
Jocelyn, studied with Stella Adler. The unstructured gifts which had been lost on
his academic teachers did not escape Stella Adler, who declared that he would
soon take a prominent place in the American theater.

A summer stock stint on Long Island followed, ending when the director,
Erwin Piscator, found Brando and a fellow actress necking. No matter — an
agent acquaintance of Adler's arranged an audition for *I Remember Mama* on
Broadway. Brando played Nels, the fifteen-year-old son, for a year. The studios
began to court him. He resisted. "They've never made an honest picture in their
lives," he is quoted as saying, "and they probably never will." Instead, he went
into a new play, *Truckline Cafe*, in 1946. The Playbill for that production stated
that Brando was born in Bangkok, where his father was stationed on a zoological
expedition. The play didn't last, but Brando did. He was immediately cast by
Guthrie McClintic in alternating plays starring his wife, Katharine Cornell —
Antigone and *Candida*.

As Stanley Kowalski in *A Streetcar Named Desire*. Warner Brothers, 1951.

With Esther Williams on the set of *Julius Caesar*. MGM, 1953.

After several other productions, he became a member of the Actors Studio. Then Elia Kazan cast him as Stanley Kowalski in *A Streetcar Named Desire*, which opened on Broadway, December 3, 1947. His "STELLLLLLAAAAAA" was heard 'round the world and reverberates today. *Streetcar* is the story of Blanche DuBois, but it was Brando's play. John Chapman wrote in his review, "Mr. Brando is magnificent as the forthright husband, in his simple rages, his simple affections and his blunt humor," while Richard Watts, Jr. wrote, "I have hitherto not shared the enthusiasm of most reviewers for Marlon Brando, but his portrayal of the heroine's sullen, violent nemesis is an excellent piece of work." Audiences and reviewers weren't used to such bold sexuality in the late '40s, such shocking animal magnetism.

Brando was committed to *Streetcar* for two years, and it was apparently during that time that he realized that the constant repetition of a role did not interest him, and that the theater was not where he belonged.

After he left *Streetcar* and took a long-desired trip to Paris, he agreed to do *The Men* (1950), a gritty, realistic story about paraplegic war veterans, for Stanley Kramer. In preparation, he lived on a paraplegic ward for four weeks. This film was followed by the controversial film version of *Streetcar* (1951). The censors insisted upon heavy cuts. Elia Kazan wrote an article about it in the *New York Times* in October 1951, explaining that the Legion of Decency was planning on giving the picture a "C" (Condemned) rating. "They at once assumed," wrote Kazan, "that no Catholic would buy a ticket." Today, these cuts seem laughable. They ranged from eliminating some music, because it made Stella's relationship to Stanley "too carnal," to omitting the words, "on the mouth," following the words, "I would like to kiss you softly and sweetly." Censors also demanded that Stanley's line, "You know, you might not be bad to interfere with," be taken out, right before he attacks Blanche. Kazan stated, "This removes the clear implication that only here, for the first time, does Stanley have any idea of harming the girl. This obviously changes the interpretation of the character, but how it serves the cause of morality is obscure to me." Nevertheless, *Streetcar* was a huge hit, and Brando was nominated for an Oscar, although he lost to Humphrey Bogart.

Brando embraced the anti-hero image off the screen as well as on. He didn't cooperate with fan magazines. He told Sidney Skolsky, "I'm tired of too many hack writers on my back." He was called "The Slob," because of the way he dressed. Hollywood simply didn't know how to handle this mold-breaking genius. It didn't have to. His work was the important thing, and it was damn good. Other Oscar nominations followed for *Viva Zapata!* (1952) and for

Julius Caesar (1953).

As a favor to Stanley Kramer, he took the part of Johnny in *The Wild One* (1954). Brando didn't like the film and said of it, "We started out to do something worthwhile, to explain the psychology of the hipster. . . Instead of finding out why young people tend to bunch into groups that seek expression in violence, all that we did was show the violence."

Jeanine Basinger wrote: "What female who was a teenager . . . escaped the mania that swept the United States in the form of Marlon Brando attached to a motorcycle? . . . We instantly recognized him as exactly what we had been waiting for in a young man — somebody really rotten." For young girls living, as she put it, "with only the dimmest possibility of time off for bad behavior," Brando represented a way out of '50s boredom.

Next was *On the Waterfront* (1954), which finally won him the Oscar. Again directed by Kazan, it told the story of a former boxer, Terry Malloy, involved in the gangster world that affected the unions.

It was at this point that, by and large, the money offered Brando for films that did not showcase his amazing talents began to be more attractive to him than challenging roles. Although he walked off the set of *The Egyptian*, for which he was offered $150,000, he had to do *Desiree* (1954) in its place in order to avoid

Brando visiting the set of *East of Eden*: Elia Kazan, Brando, Julie Harris, James Dean. Warner Brothers, 1955.

On the set of *The Young Lions*: Montgomery Clift, Marlon Brando and Dean Martin. 20th Century Fox, 1958.

a lawsuit against him by 20th Century Fox. (Later, he fulfilled the rest of his commitment by doing *The Young Lions* in 1958.) Brando called playing Napoleon ". . . the most shaming experience of my life." He sang and was successful in *Guys and Dolls* (1955) and won another Oscar nomination for *Sayonara* (1957). *The Young Lions* was the last money-making film Brando did, until *The Godfather* in 1972. He directed and starred in *One Eyed Jacks* (1960).

After his unsuccessful portrayal of Fletcher Christian in *Mutiny on the Bounty* (1962), the downhill slide began. This was in no small part due to an article about the film published in the *Saturday Evening Post*, called "The Mutiny of Marlon Brando," over which Brando sued the Curtis Publishing Company for five million dollars. The suit did not come to court, but there is no doubt that Brando was harmed by the article.

Some of Brando's subsequent films and/or performances received good reviews, but many of the films were either unsuccessful at the box office or not widely released. *The Ugly American* (1963), *Bedtime Story* (1964), *The Saboteur* (1965), *Reflections in a Golden Eye* (1967) and *Candy* (1968) are some examples. Basically, he settled in Tahiti and stayed there.

Brando, however, was anxious to do *The Godfather* (1972). Paramount agreed to his casting on the conditions that he take a percentage of the profits and no salary, and that he post a bond to insure against delays he himself might cause. The studio executives dropped their demand for a bond when they saw the impressive test of Brando as Don Vito Corleone, shown to them by the film's director, Francis Ford Coppola. Brando's extraordinary, now often imitated, characterization won him another Oscar. Unlike 1955, when he won for *On the Waterfront*, Brando did not appear at the Oscars. In his place, he sent an Indian, Sasheen Littlefeather, to protest the way the American Indian had been portrayed in film. In his statement, he said that he was going to Wounded Knee instead of the Oscar ceremony. He didn't show up at Wounded Knee, either.

"I want to act in French movies," Brando once said. "In French pictures, you can live, make love, do everything that people really do." *Last Tango in Paris* (1973) fulfilled those criteria for him, but almost too much. After improvising speeches and exposing so much of himself, literally as well as figuratively, he told Bertolucci, "I have felt a violation of my innermost self." Nevertheless, he received another Oscar nomination.

For twelve days' work on *Superman* (1978), Brando, as Jor-El, Superman's father, allegedly received $4 million. His beautiful farewell speech to the baby Superman makes one sigh with regret. We have seen too little of this man. He appears at the end of *Apocalypse Now* (1979) as Kurtz, a man talked about constantly throughout the film. How like Brando — talked about, but not there. His appearances have been few and far between since then. *The Freshman* in 1990 was his last. He is scheduled to appear in October 1992 in *Christopher Columbus: The Discovery*.

Marlon Brando could have been a contender, and for a time, he was. But mostly what he has done as he's aged is a last tango with our souls, giving us hopeful glimpses of an ever-ebbing light.

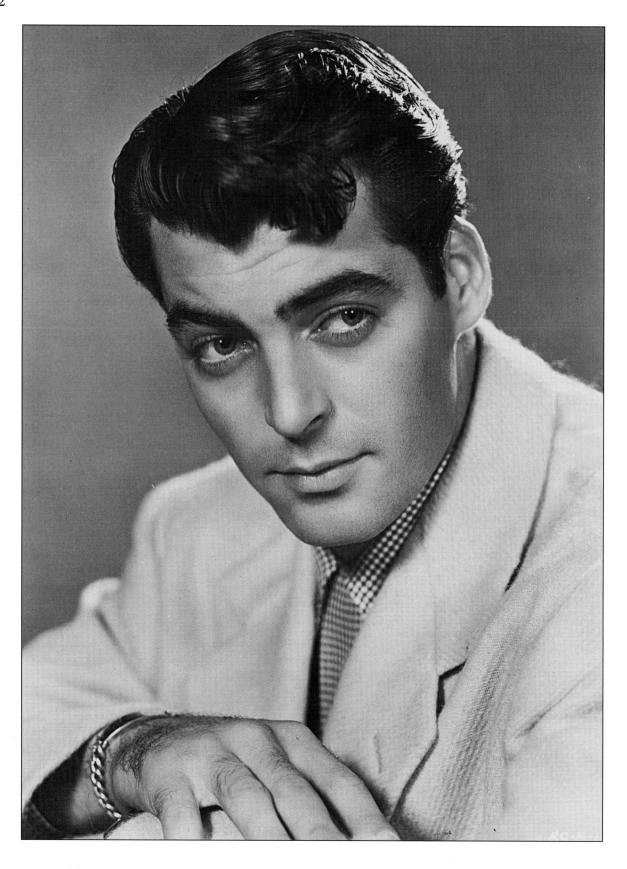

Rory Calhoun
A Little Bad

Back in the '50s, celebrities feared *Confidential*, one of a few tell-all publications that portrayed a seamier side of Hollywood than did the studio-oriented fan magazines. One February day in 1955, readers of *Confidential* opened the magazine to this headline: MOVIE STAR RORY CALHOUN: BUT FOR THE GRACE OF GOD STILL A CONVICT! Above the headline, on the left, was the Salt Lake City mug shot of a 1940 Calhoun, back in the days when his eyebrows joined at his nose, and on the right, a publicity portrait of the handsome actor. His entire police record, mostly juvenile auto offenses, as well as his aliases, appeared on the next page. (One of the more scandalous tidbits from the article: "'Come on kid,' [a tough schoolmate said to him], 'I'll show you how to get your own bubble gum' . . . Rory learned how to crack open a gum machine.")

How *Confidential* obtained Calhoun's record has been a subject of speculation over the years. Supposedly, Calhoun's story was traded for one on the sex life of the more important Rock Hudson. Maybe.

At any rate, it wasn't enough to hurt Calhoun's career, which was not truly of the top rank. He was, however, ruggedly handsome and macho, and found a nice home not only in films, but television.

Francis Timothy McCown was born in Los Angeles on August 8, 1922. Some time after his father's death, his mother married a man named Durgin. Calhoun grew up during the Depression in a slum and, after being caught for petty theft, was sent to a home for disturbed children. He escaped from there by hot-wiring a car with a friend. His next stop was a reformatory. Paroled to the custody of his parents, he soon was in the "hot car racket," using the name of Jack Raine. He was sent to prison in Salt Lake City following an aborted jewelry store robbery. After turning his hot car confederates in to the FBI, he was sent to a reformatory in Reno, Oklahoma, at the end of which he was due to spend twenty years in San Quentin.

At El Reno Federal Reformatory, he met Father Don J. Kanally, who baptized him in the men's washroom and helped Calhoun turn things around for himself. In 1975, Calhoun told writer David Ragan, "He [Kanally] taught me values I hadn't learned as a youngster . . . And I hope that anyone who needs a helping hand will be as lucky as I was in having a Father Kanally." Kanally, along with Calhoun's mother and stepfather, managed to get the charges against him in California dropped, so that when he was finally released from the reformatory, he was free.

Calhoun then worked at a steel mill, later as a lumberjack and a forester. In January 1944, he returned to Los Angeles to visit his mother. Renting a horse and riding in the San Fernando hills, he met a rider, who, impressed with Calhoun's stature, looks and voice, suggested he might try the movies. He invited the young Calhoun to dinner. It was then that Calhoun learned he was talking to Alan Ladd, and Ladd's wife, of course, was the influential agent Sue Carol.

Carol arranged for a test at Twentieth Century Fox. As Fred McCowan, he had a small role in *Something for the Boys* (1944). Later, David Selznick changed his name to Rory Calhoun — "Rory" because, as a forest ranger, Calhoun had put out roaring blazes, and "Calhoun" because Selznick thought it sounded more Irish than McCowan. Other small parts followed. By 1950, he was able to get a good role in *A Ticket To Tomahawk*, followed by *I'd Climb the Highest Mountain* (1951), *With A Song in My Heart* (1952) and *Powder River* (1953). He played Betty Grable's love interest — and a forest ranger — in *How to Marry a Millionaire* (1953) and a gambler in *River of No Return* (1954), which starred Marilyn Monroe and Robert Mitchum.

Western upon western followed: *Guns to the Border* (1954), *Dawn at Socorro* (1954), *Treasure of Pancho Villa* (1955), *The Hired Gun* (1957), and many others. From 1958-1960, he appeared in his own television series, "The Texan."

With Lauren Bacall, Betty Grable and Marilyn Monroe in *How to Marry a Millionaire*.
20th Century Fox, 1953.

Eventually, he became a television mainstay, guest-starring on many shows: "Petrocelli," "Owen Marshall," "Alias Smith and Jones," and others. From 1970-72, following a bitter, messy divorce from his wife of twenty-one years, Lita Baron, with whom he had three daughters, he did not work by choice. He told the *New York Times*, "I figured the more I worked, the more alimony I had to pay her. So I stayed idle." (Calhoun remarried in 1971, and he and his new wife had a daughter, Rory, that same year.) In his later career, there have been some questionable films, such as *Motel Hell* (1980), co-starring Wolfman Jack ("Good to see Rory and Wolfman sharing screen credit," Leonard Maltin wrote), and *Angel* (1984), and a soap opera, "Capitol."

Rory Calhoun persevered in his career in spite of not only *Confidential*, but also, before the story broke, blackmail attempts from ex-cellmates. He told Maurice Zolotow in 1955, "Let the whole story come out. At least, I wouldn't have to live in continual fear of a telephone ringing and a hoarse voice whispering, 'This is a friend of yours from El Reno, Rory.'"

Further indication of his spunk is evidenced by a statement he made to the *New York Times* regarding the charge by Lita Baron that he committed adultery with 79 women. "Heck, she didn't include even half of them."

Jeff Chandler
A Lion's Shadow

Jeff Chandler wasn't Hollywood's idea of a leading man when he burst onto the scene. Rugged, 6'4" and prematurely gray in an era of smooth, young looks, he soon proved he had star quality. Unfortunately, what might have been an interesting career was cut short by his horrific death at the age of forty-two.

"Jeff Chandler" was really Ira Grossel from Brooklyn, born December 15, 1918. Although he wanted to be an actor from early youth, a talent for art led him to art school. Later, a fellow student there brought him to the Feagin School of Dramatic Arts, where in exchange for working at the school, he was given a scholarship.

Had Chandler been more conventional-looking, he would have been plucked from obscurity years earlier than he was. His good friend and eventual agent, Meyer Mishkin, first saw Chandler perform in New York in 1940. "I had seen him in a play in Maplewood, New Jersey, in stock. At that time, I was a talent scout for Twentieth Century Fox, and all we were looking for were leading men — the leading men would look like Ty Power. Well, I went backstage and talked to Jeff. I said, 'I'll remember you, because you're very good, but we're just not looking for your kind of guy.' Too rugged!"

After serving in the Army, Chandler, in 1945, headed for Hollywood with

In *Iron Man*. Universal, 1951.

$3,000 he'd saved. He changed his name to Jeff Chandler — Chandler after Van Johnson's character in *Easy to Wed* and Jeff at the suggestion of actor Gerald Mohr. As he told New York reporter Dorothy Masters in 1949, "I spent $1,000 on clothes and waited for 11 producers to fall on their faces over my arrival. In three months, when the bankroll was about gone, I said, 'look here, chum, gotta buckle down.'" He found steady work in radio, where his rich voice stood him in good stead. Ultimately, he was chosen to play Eve Arden's boyfriend, Mr. Boynton, on the "Our Miss Brooks" radio program.

Re-enter Meyer Mishkin. By this time, Mishkin was no longer at Fox and on his own as an agent. "A friend of mine, Sam Jaffe, asked me if I would go and see an actor who was in a show called "Our Miss Brooks," which was a very important radio show. It seemed that Jeff's radio agent at the time was going out of business.

"I looked at him, and I thought to myself, 'that's not Jeff Chandler. That's Ira Grossel.' This time, since I was making my own decisions, I told him I would be very happy to represent him. He said he'd love it.

"We talked about it later — I came home and said to my wife, 'Well, I met an actor today I knew in New York, and I think he can become a star.' Jeff went home and said to his wife, 'I met an agent today I think I can have a career with.'

"We were fortunate. He did a few small parts in films [his first film was *Johnny O'Clock* in 1947]. Then, they were doing a film at Universal called *Sword in the Desert* (1949) about the Israeli war. I spoke to the casting director at Universal, whom I had known for a number of years, and he said, 'Gee, he might be an idea as the leader of the Israelis.' Naturally! We were talking about someone whose real name was Ira Grossel! So they tested him, and that's how he starred in *Sword in the Desert*." Not that Chandler's billing exactly pleased him. "In Hollywood," he told Dorothy Masters, "they consider it the kiss of death when your credit line begins with 'And introducing . . .'"

After *Sword in the Desert* was released and doing well, Mishkin was able to interest Twentieth Century Fox in casting Chandler as Cochise in *Broken Arrow* (1950). By this time, Chandler was under contract to Universal, so Fox borrowed him.

Broken Arrow earned Jeff Chandler a supporting Oscar nomination and established him in Hollywood. Unfortunately, excellent films didn't follow, and today, *Broken Arrow* stands alone on Chandler's filmography as a great film. The reason? "The problem," Meyer Mishkin said, "was that he was still under one of those seven-year contracts to Universal. He had to be in the pictures that Universal was doing at that time. If you were under contract for Universal, you made a lot of films that weren't good, but were just being turned out. . . It put actors on a certain level. They weren't considered the way they should have been in relation to the actor's growth in stature. They were considered as to the actor's value to the studio, so the studio didn't have to hire outside actors."

Universal refused to lend Chandler out for *The Day the Earth Stood Still* (1951), *The Secret of Convict Lake* (1951) and *Les Miserables* (1952). Instead, he did *The Iron Man* (1951), *Flame of Araby* (1951), *The Battle of Apache Pass* (1952) and *The Great Sioux Uprising* (1953). In 1954, he made *Sign of the Pagan*. His co-star, Rita Gam, remembers him as "a very darling man, a very generous-spirited, witty man who kept bowls of bubble gum on his dressing room table for everyone to share. It may have been a sign of the times, I'm not sure. Today, I have known movie stars to have bowls of coke on their table.

"We had a great buddy friendship, like brother and sister, and we practiced our sword fights for the film together every day between five and six.

As Cochise with James Stewart in *Broken Arrow*. 20th Century Fox, 1950.

Chandler and friend Tony Curtis.

Chandler with family, 1953.

"I think he started out being an actor who wanted a serious career and got trapped in the mode of the time, which was the adventure film. There wasn't much he could have done about that. He was wonderful, you know. His death was really heart-breaking, at the height of his career."

Jeff Chandler's later films were a bit better, as he negotiated a lucrative and less restrictive contract with Universal, which gave him an opportunity to work for other studios. He was the gigolo Joan Crawford flipped for in *The Female on the Beach* (1955), Jeanne Crain's wandering attorney husband in the courtroom potboiler *The Tattered Dress* (1957), Kim Novak's sexy boyfriend in *Jeanne Eagels* (1957), and Lana Turner's pilot husband in *The Lady Takes a Flyer* (1958). For *Eagels*, Columbia Pictures paid him $200,000. Chandler told Sheilah Graham, "I thought for once I could keep my shirt on and not have to shave my chest. But today, for a man to be a hit on the screen, he has to take his shirt off." He and Meyer Mishkin formed a production company, Earlmar Productions, and Chandler signed a recording contract with Decca Records, for which he recorded "I Should Care" and "More Than Anyone." He took his singing career even further, doing an act at the Riviera Hotel in Las Vegas.

Chandler had made thirty-seven films, when he traveled to the Philippines to do what would be his last film, *Merrill's Marauders* (1961). At the time he left for location, his back was bothering him, and when he returned, the pain had worsened. He decided to check into a hospital to be operated on for a slipped disk. (Today, surgery is not normally required for a slipped disk.) He called Meyer Mishkin and said, "When I come out, we'll have dinner." Chandler never left the hospital.

On May 13, 1961, the operation took place. It is alleged that at that time, the surgeon possibly nicked Chandler's aorta, which caused hemorrhaging. On May 18, the actor was rushed into emergency surgery for bleeding, receiving fifty-five pints of blood during a seven-hour operation. A third operation took place on May 27th. He died on June 17th. During the last week of his life, he was in such pain that he begged to die.

Chandler's death certificate listed the cause of death as shock, and as contributing causes: a staphylococcal infection, pneumonia and bone marrow suppression. There were also details given regarding a fourth operation, this one for gall bladder inflammation. Outraged members of the Screen Actors Guild, led by actor Clint Walker, signed a petition and demanded that a fact-finding committee delve into the circumstances of Chandler's death.

As part of a $1.8 million lawsuit filed on behalf of Chandler's two children, the hospital settled out of court, canceling the doctor and hospital bills and placing a little over $200,000 in trust for Chandler's daughters.

Jeff Chandler didn't leave a legacy of classic films, but he was attractive, likable and very popular, both with the public and people who knew him in the industry. Fellow Universalite Tony Curtis, who served as a pall bearer at Chandler's funeral, said Jeff Chandler was "the best of men." His end shouldn't have been so cruel, or so soon.

Montgomery Clift
An Antic Disposition

On a recent episode of *Biography* profiling Montgomery Clift, the series host, Peter Graves, said: "[Clift's] life plays like a terrible Greek tragedy." Indeed, so did that particular episode of *Biography*.

And yet, Montgomery Clift's very good friend, Jack Larson, claims that the problem with the Clift books, and with just about everything having to do with Clift, is the determination to make him a tragic figure. "There were a handful of us," Larson said, "that were very close to Monty, and we loved being with him. He wasn't a depressing creature, even after the accident. He was always a joy to be with. He never laid anything on anyone. He was essentially very 'up' and vital, full of humor and brilliance."

Monty's lover, Libby Holman (Clift also had male lovers), called Clift's penchant for practical jokes his "divine madness." "He'd do things that were terribly, terribly funny," Larson continued. "He was nearer to Jerry Lewis in his sense of humor. When people would see him like that, they'd think he was drunk or something, and he wasn't. I'm not saying he didn't drink, but there was no relationship between what he was like on screen and as a friend, and his screen persona, serious and romantic."

"A man don't go his own way, he's nothin'," Clift's character, Prewitt, says in

From Here to Eternity. And the headstrong, sexually ambivalent Clift most definitely went his own way from the very beginning. He was born Edward Montgomery Clift on October 17, 1920 (along with his twin, Roberta), in Omaha, Nebraska. His education, organized by his strong-willed mother, Sunny, was somewhat unconventional and included a good deal of European travel. It was the family tutor, Walter Hayward, who arranged the audition for Monty's first role at the age of twelve in an amateur production of *As Husbands Go* in Sarasota, Florida. In 1933, the family moved to New York City.

Broadway followed: *Fly Away Home* in 1935, *Your Obedient Husband*, starring Frederic March and Florence Eldridge in 1938, *There Shall Be No Night* with the Lunts in 1940, *The Skin of Our Teeth* in 1942, *Our Town* in 1944, and many others.

Hollywood began to woo him for the first time in 1941. As Jack Larson tells it, "Monty had done *There Shall Be No Night* on Broadway and was offered the son in *Mrs. Miniver.* But he would have had to sign a long-term contract at MGM, and he wouldn't. Everybody thought he was very foolish. He never regretted it. He would never sign for anything beyond the picture and the director at hand." Later in the '40s, Clift's agent, Leland Hayward, insisted he give Hollywood a real try (Clift sent correspondence to friends with "Vomit, California" as the return address) and secured for him a six-month contract with MGM. Unable to be convinced of the wisdom of the seven-year contract, he returned to New York.

Clift, however, liked film director Howard Hawks, and especially the idea of being cast against type, so in 1947, he returned to Hollywood to make *Red River* with John Wayne. Now he was in Hollywood on his terms: a one-picture deal.

This certainly wasn't the Hollywood strategy in the '50s — it's more like the strategy today. "Yes," Larson agreed. "He picked his own material. But he was good at it. The people that are around now are not so good at it."

Clift's take on publicity wasn't exactly the Hollywood strategy of the time, either. As Larson put it, "He didn't want to lie to people. He didn't want people to think he was something he wasn't." Clift once was approached by an interviewer and, after meeting him, agreed to give him a story and be on the cover of a magazine. When the interview was published, Clift was appalled. "The handle," as he referred to it, was "Young Man with a Dream." He objected strenuously to people being fed that kind of "pap" and felt betrayed by the title. "I don't have a dream," he told Larson. "All I want to do is have good work to do, get up in the morning and go to it, come home with a good tired, and have

Clift as a young actor in *You Touched Me* (1945) on Broadway
with Edmund Gwenn and Catharine Willard.

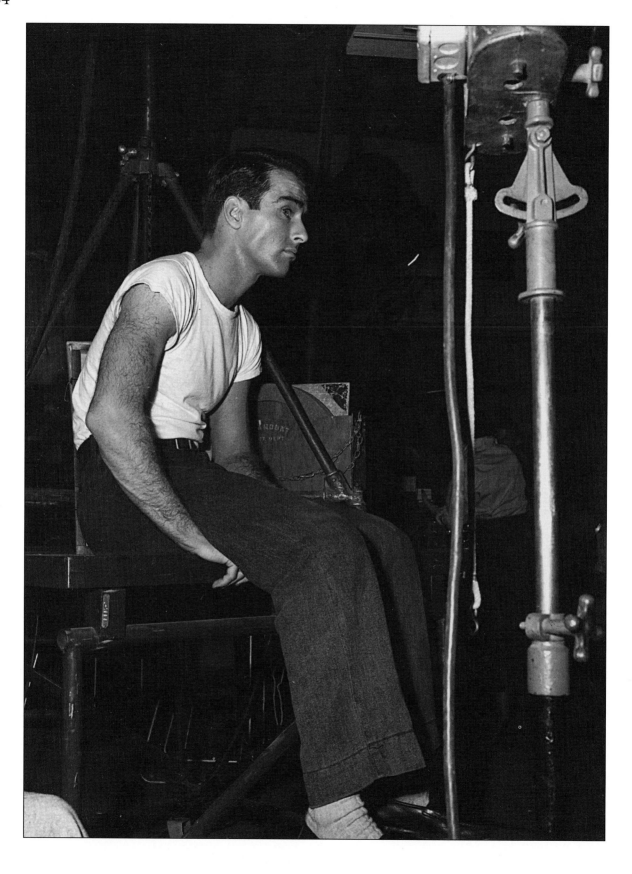

a good night's sleep — if you can call that a dream."

Clift made seventeen films, but a whole other career could have been built on what he turned down: *Shane, Sunset Boulevard, On the Waterfront,* for starters. But he claimed not to regret his decisions. Says Larson, "He turned down *Sunset Boulevard,* felt he was right to turn it down, that William Holden was better than he would have been. He liked and admired George Stevens, but Stevens photographed things from so many angles, that Monty would have found it too exhausting to do *Shane* — he felt he didn't have the stamina to be able to collaborate and give the kind of performance he wanted in another George Stevens film."

The one George Stevens film he did, *A Place in the Sun* (1951), was a classic and the first teaming of Clift and his dear friend Elizabeth Taylor. "Are they watching us?" she asks, as she and Clift dance in the film. Boy, were they ever! Who can forget the electricity between them? Clift's youthful passion and his offbeat presence dominate the film. Yet, eight years later, eyes glazed over, speech unsteady, he stares out at us in *Summer and Smoke* and breaks our hearts with what has been lost.

With Elizabeth Taylor. Photo credit: © Globe Photos.

"It was very sad what happened after the accident," Larson said, speaking of the 1956 car accident that left Clift shattered. "It was brutal. He was treated by doctors, given medicine that was not good. What can we say?" Clift insisted on returning to work on *Raintree County* after only six weeks of recuperation. "Libby felt he should quit the film and spend time healing with the best possible doctors," Larson commented. "He stayed, and a lot of things went wrong. Monty was very brave, but it was difficult for him, and I didn't feel he was medically well taken care of. But you can't think about him in those terms."

Think instead of his brilliant performances in *Wild River* (1960), *The Misfits* (1961) and *Judgment at Nuremberg* (1961). But what might have been still haunts: *Hamlet*, which he could recite flawlessly (he wanted to star in it with Myrna Loy as Gertrude and Peter Finch as Claudius); *Reflections in a Golden Eye*, starring with Elizabeth Taylor — the films he never lived to do. He was found dead in his home on July 23, 1966. The autopsy report stated he died from coronary occlusive disease. But Montgomery Clift had been dying for a long time.

Devastating health problems killed his body — never his wonderful spirit. In one of his early films, *The Search*, Clift tells the young boy his mother is gone, but will be with him "always." Clift reads the line "all ways." So is he with us, always and in all ways.

Clift as he appeared in *Suddenly Last Summer*. Columbia Pictures, 1959.

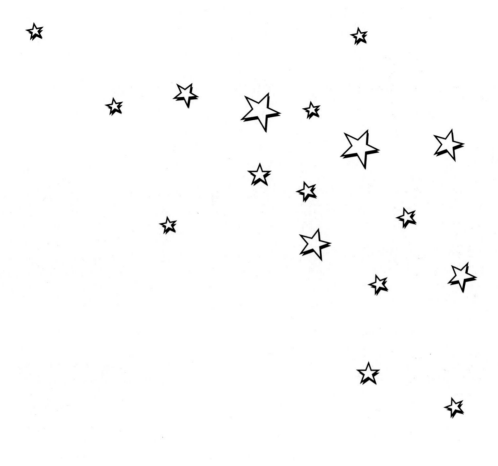

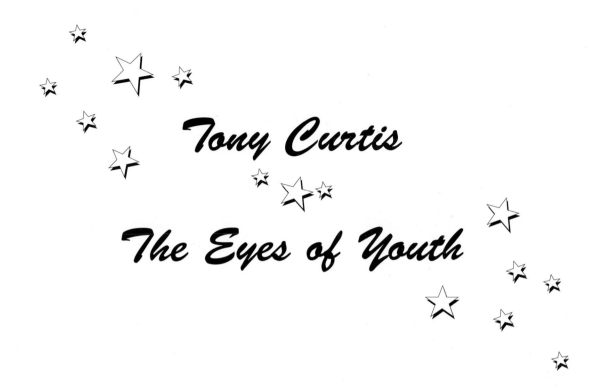

Tony Curtis
The Eyes of Youth

It is 1949. The movie is *Criss Cross*. At the beginning of the film, for a history-making 20 seconds, Yvonne de Carlo dances with a young man — then billed as one "James Curtis."

The decision of the young girls viewing *Criss Cross* was quick and unanimous. They wanted to see more — lots more — of the sexy, dark hunk who danced with Yvonne. Universal responded immediately. Curtis made over twelve films in the next three years.

Bernie Schwartz, aka James Curtis aka Anthony Curtis aka Tony Curtis, was spotted by a talent scout from Universal while performing the title role in *Golden Boy* with the Cherry Lane Players in Greenwich Village. So off he went to Hollywood, briefly rooming with Marlon Brando when he first arrived.

After the prepubescent females noticed the new actor in *Criss Cross*, Universal gave him a role as a hoodlum in *City Across the River* (1949). Agent Meyer Mishkin has this story to tell about Bernie Schwartz's various name changes: "I had only been an agent out here for a few months when I bumped into Bernie Schwartz on the Universal lot. I knew him from New York. I said, 'What are you doing here?' He said, 'I'm under contract. They signed me.' I said, 'Gee, that's great.' He said, 'They changed my name.' Naturally. 'What are they calling you?'

'James Curtis.' I said, 'You're no James.' I went in to see a director-producer who was making *City Across the River* about Jersey City. And I said to him, 'You know, you've got a kid under contract here who'd be very good in the picture, but they call him James Curtis. He's no James. You've got to change his name.'" For whatever reason, soon the film credits said, "Anthony Curtis," and then "Tony Curtis."

Why did they change his name from Anthony to Tony? "Well," Curtis told me, "it wasn't actually changed. We just shortened it to Tony as the movies went on. I met somebody in New York once, and she looked at me and said, 'Tony of the movies.' From then on, I thought it would be best to be called Tony." More boyish, no doubt.

When his fan mail increased, Universal did what they always did with their glamour boys — moved him into period pieces. Soon, audiences were seeing "Tony Curtis" in *The Prince Who Was a Thief* (1951), *Son of Ali Baba* (1952) and *The Black Shield of Falworth* (1954), Bronx accent and all. These films were a far cry from later Curtis movies. "But you know," he said, "I would have been different. Listen, it was just a matter of what kind of movies I got. If they would have taken me and not put me in the *Son of Ali Baba* and *The Prince Who Was a Thief* and let me play some young man out of New York City striving for some kind of success, you would have seen all that in me a lot earlier. But they didn't.

With Janet Leigh in *The Perfect Furlough*. Universal, 1959.

Tony Curtis and Piper Laurie in *Son of Ali Baba*. Universal, 1952.

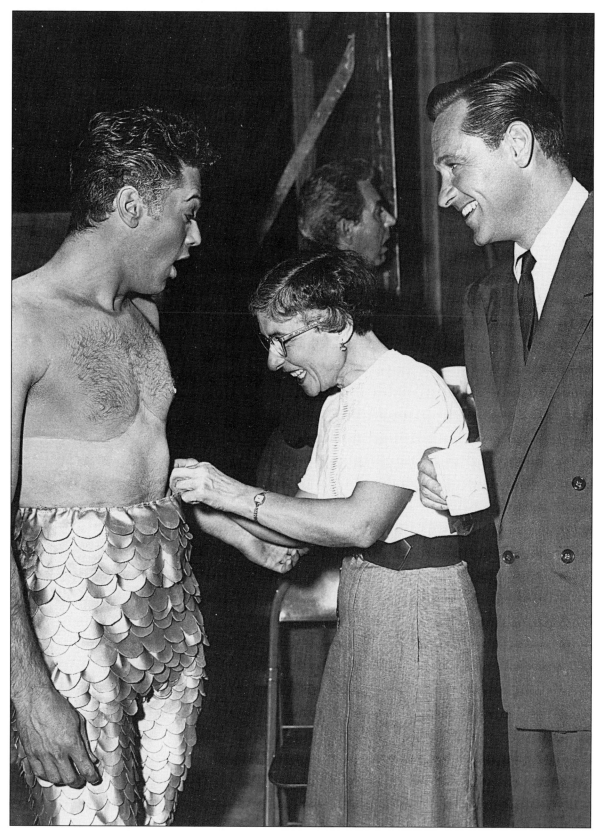

On the set of *Houdini* with William Holden. Paramount, 1953.

Marlon, because of his beginnings in the theater, was able to get *The Men* and *Streetcar Named Desire*. They wouldn't have dared give him the *Son of Ali Baba*! Since I didn't have that kind of credibility or those credentials, they put me in those other movies and were kind of stunned I was able to play better parts."

In Tony's case, however, it wasn't just a lack of experience that kept him from getting important roles. Let's face it — Brando was very good-looking and sexy, but Tony Curtis had real movie-star, juvenile looks, and the studio, understandably, capitalized on them.

Okay — to have Tony Curtis play a young hoodlum seemed reasonable. But what was the purpose of the swashbuckling strategy the studio followed?

"Universal would do it with anybody. They didn't have anybody who knew how to make other than those kinds of movies — swashbuckling, Maria Montez, Jon Hall films. They were geared for that. They had the sets built earlier and the costumes made for the Sabu movies, so it was a natural spring from there. They did it with anybody who was under contract."

Did Universal set up competition between Curtis and another young hunk, Rock Hudson?

"No, we all worked together. But they normally did set up competition. When they signed me, they put under contract three or four guys that looked not unlike me. And when Rock joined them, they put on a couple of guys who looked like Rock. They did that so that if you became difficult, they would be able to wave somebody in front of you and say, 'Listen, if we did it with you, we can do it with anyone'."

Like all young players under the studio system, Tony dutifully went to classes. One in particular stood out — "the kissing class. I was the instructor. I got up in front of the girls and said, 'I've been assigned by Universal to teach girls how to kiss.'" He also remembers Sophie Rosenstein, the gifted drama coach. "A big talent. She was magnificent — receding chin, odd little woman. I really enjoyed her company and the essence that she gave."

With his dark hair, dreamy blue eyes and killer smile, the fans couldn't get enough of him. Was the adulation difficult to handle? With characteristic candor, Tony replied, "No. I've had that all my life, before I got into the movies. In school, in the neighborhoods, wherever I lived, there was always a furor. I felt that, anyway. Everybody liked the way I looked, including myself. I was a nice-looking boy with a nice smile, and there wasn't anything salacious or weird about it. So when I got into the movies and it started happening there, it was just a little larger, but I was somewhat used to it."

And what about the interminable publicity? (In 1958, *Photoplay* magazine named him the most popular star among movie fans.) "I only started to dislike the fan magazines when I divorced my first wife [Janet Leigh], and they kept putting articles entitled, 'Tony, Come Home — Your Daughters Miss You' and 'Why Did you Abandon Your Children?' And when that started happening, I stopped reading the movie magazines."

Leaving Universal in the late '50s, he was able to graduate from the teen-idol category, with fine performances in films that matched his ability: *Sweet Smell of Success* (1957), *The Defiant Ones* (1958, for which he received an Oscar nomination), *Operation Petticoat* (1959) and *Some Like It Hot* (1959). Like another Universal graduate, Rock Hudson, he found a place in comedy and wasn't above self-mockery, as demonstrated by his performance in *The Great Race* (1965).

Today, Curtis concentrates on his stunning art work as well as his acting (*Christmas in Connecticut* in 1992). He is also preparing his upcoming autobiography. He looks back on his long and successful career — and, given his former drug and alcohol problem, his own physical survival — with something akin to awe. Like most successful performers, he was too busy living his life to realize the great cinematic footprints he was leaving. I reminded him of a recent film set in the '50s, *Let 'Em Have It*, where all the kids are excited, because they're going to see a Tony Curtis movie. "How happy I am," he said, "but not as excited as I am when *I* see a Tony Curtis movie." Every young boy wanted to be Tony Curtis.

"Including," he observed, "Tony Curtis."

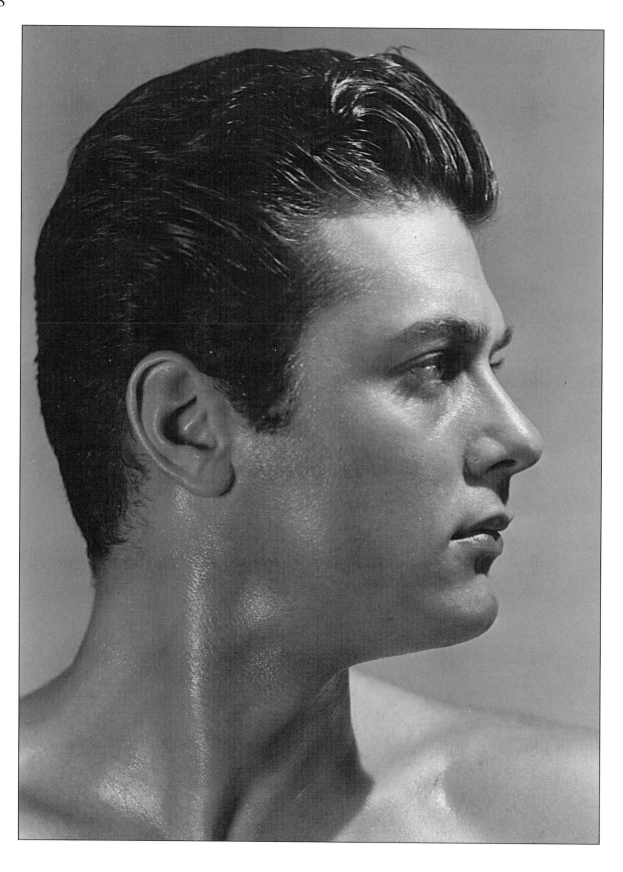

James Dean

How Brief the Life

In 1985, while traveling in Europe, I found James Dean everywhere, as if he were a brand-new movie star and hadn't been dead for thirty years. His movies were on television (and European television, it should be noted, doesn't run films with anywhere near the same frequency as U.S. television, nor are there as many channels). Life-sized cutouts of him adorned clothing store windows. On the street, artists sketched his picture, and teenagers fell over themselves, yelling, "James Dean!" to get a closer look. A German magazine ran an article about him, and the ensuing letters to the editor ran on for a dozen pages.

Jack Larson, who knew Dean briefly in his early New York days, laughs a bit at Dean's image as a rebel. "I take nothing away from him. He was a brilliant actor, photogenic, deserves every bit of praise. But he was doing a bit — it was very clear. These kids now, I feel so bad for them, they base so much on being a rebel. They're all rebels against publicity and against photographers — it's typical of a certain attitude towards performing that's based on Jimmy Dean. Supposedly, he was a great rebel.

"Nobody, not even Marilyn Monroe, was more photographed than James Dean! Sandy Roth, a photographer, was behind him in a car the day Dean died and photographed the wreck. When Jimmy Dean returned to his home town, something which would normally be a private thing, he took Bob Willoughby, a photographer, with him. He was photographed anywhere, and he never quit being photographed. Then he'd say, 'Oh, I hate it, I hate it. I'm a rebel.' It was a tactic. Maybe he believed it, maybe he got into it. But nobody cooperated with the press more than Jimmy Dean, cooperated to the hilt. That included Hedda Hopper. Montgomery Clift did not cooperate and would not do many interviews — there you see someone who really meant it. These kids now act like rebels and knock cameras out of photographers' hands. I always think, 'Gee, you'll be sorry they didn't take that picture one day.'"

Whether Dean was or was not a rebel in his private life, whether or not he was really that tortured young man we saw up on the screen, the magic of his persona has been working on the public for nearly forty years, with his legend growing deeper and stronger as time passes. But then, time only passes for mere mortals. James Dean is no longer one of those.

James Byron Dean was born February 8, 1931, in Marion, Indiana. Dean was five when his father, a dental technician, was put on staff at a Los Angeles veteran's hospital, so the family moved west. His mother, who loved music, had her son trained in the violin. She died a slow, painful death from cancer when Dean was nine. When he became a star, Dean, in a rush of pent-up emotion, told an interviewer, "My mother died on me when I was nine years old. What does she expect me to do? Do it all by myself?"

Dean was sent back to Indiana to live with his grandmother, uncle and aunt. There, he enjoyed a sense of family, popularity in school and achieved scholastic and athletic excellence. In 1949, he became a pre-law student, working as a radio announcer at the college radio station. He eventually left for the theater program at UCLA.

From connections made in college, he began to get acting work. One of his first jobs was in a cola commercial with Nick Adams. He then played John the Baptist in a television drama, "Hill Number One," and worked in radio. Hopelessly bitten by the acting bug, he left college. His good friend, William Bast, helped him meet a radio director, who advised him about getting bits in films and hired him for small parts on the radio. In his first four films, he played bit roles: *Sailor Beware* (1951), *Fixed Bayonets* (1951), *Has Anybody Seen My Gal?* (1952) and *Trouble Along the Way* (1953). In between his acting work, he ushered at CBS and worked as a parking lot attendant.

One of his advisors at the time was actor James Whitmore, of whom Dean once said, "I owe a lot to him . . . He told me I didn't know the difference between acting as a soft job and acting as a difficult art." When Dean made the decision to move to New York and get into television, Whitmore encouraged him.

East of Eden. Warner Brothers, 1955.

With Natalie Wood on the set of *Rebel Without a Cause*. Warner Brothers, 1955.

In New York, he worked odd jobs and came to the attention of an agent, Jane Deacy. She helped him gain the experience he needed. He sat in on acting sessions at the Actors Studio and allegedly walked out after being harshly critiqued for a reading. A Broadway play, *See the Jaguar*, followed in 1952, as did a multitude of television appearances, the most notable of which was "A Long Time Till Dawn" on "Kraft Theatre," which was his first starring role. He also appeared on the "Robert Montgomery Presents," "Philco Playhouse" and "Danger" television series.

After success on Broadway in *The Immoralist* (1954), his agent fought to win him a screen test for *East of Eden*. The rest is cinematic history. Based on part of Steinbeck's sweeping modern-day Cain and Abel story, *Eden* was tailor-made for Dean's talents. The image of him huddled on top of a train haunts to this day as a symbol of alienation. "I gotta know who I am, I gotta know what I'm like," he agonizes in the film. Teenagers of any era, not to mention those post-war, could relate to Aaron's anger and confusion, his curiosity about the adult world. "Talk to me, please," he begs Jo Van Fleet, who plays his mother. Certainly the most compelling scene in the film is the one in which he viscerally cries out like a wounded animal for his stern father's (Raymond Massey) love, clutching Massey's solid, implacable frame. It tears at the heart.

The combination of introvert and extrovert is what makes Dean interesting on film. He mumbles and slouches one minute; the next, he breaks into a dimpled smile that lights up his entire face, and his laugh is infectious. The combination made him interesting in person, too, as mentioned by Jack Larson. He was much photographed and interviewed, but considered difficult to work with, because of the careful, analytical, soul-searching work he did. Raymond Massey complained that everybody on the set of *Eden* had to wait for Dean to be ready. Well, the results were worth it. Dean and the director, Elia Kazan (who never cared for Dean and called him a creep), were nominated for Oscars.

Realizing what they had in Dean, Warner Brothers wasted no time in readying *Rebel Without a Cause* (1955). Directed by Nicholas Ray, the film was significant in its portrayal of well-to-do juvenile delinquents, instead of the disadvantaged ones Hollywood usually portrayed. The drama in it is heavy, the script talky, but Dean fascinates, leading a cast that connects and sparks.

Of Dean's ability to cope with his huge success, *Look* magazine writer George Sculli wrote later, "Dean was only too eager to be overwhelmed . . . he read avidly every word of his build-up, especially those that compared him to Marlon Brando." As *East of Eden* was completed and *Rebel Without a Cause* began, Dean began to dress sloppily, to be insulting to interviewers, behavior apparently

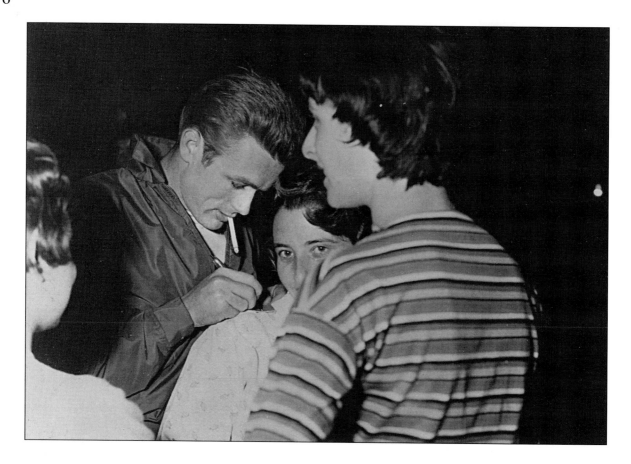

modeled on what he knew of Brando.

As Warner's worked up a lucrative contract for Dean, plans were being made to loan him out to MGM for *Somebody Up There Likes Me* and *Fear Strikes Out*. He was also being considered for *Damn Yankees* at Warner Brothers. After Alan Ladd turned down Jett Rink in *Giant*, Warner's assigned the role to Dean. It was not an assignment Dean particularly wanted.

By the time *Giant* was released, Dean was dead. Needless to say, the film was a huge hit. Jett Rink was Dean's least successful role, however, particularly at the end of the film, when, in atrocious make-up, he plays the aged Jett.

On September 30, 1955, Dean was traveling to Salinas to take part in a car race, when his silver Porsche sportscar crashed into another car. Dean was killed almost instantly. He was buried next to his mother in Fairmount, Indiana, eight days later.

As often happens when a popular person dies, fans unable to accept the event react strongly, and the more tabloid-oriented media aid and abet them. Dean was alive, some rumors began, but living as a vegetable, mutilated beyond

recognition. Magazines carried headlines to the effect that Dean was appearing to his fans, giving them messages from the beyond. Because it was a less avaricious time, the thousands of old girlfriends who came forward didn't get book deals, but were able to sell their stories for sometimes as much as $25. Tons of memorabilia went on sale, as did many recordings: "Hymn for James Dean," "Jimmy Dean Is Not Dead," "Jimmy, Jimmy," and others. The Porsche, the instrument of death, went on tour. A film, *The James Dean Story*, was released in 1957.

Despite attempts to cheapen and commercialize his memory, the integrity of Dean's image and work lives on and continues to speak to people all over the world, especially the youth to whom he was such a symbol. If he had lived, James Dean would be sixty-one years old. It's not only impossible to imagine him at that age, it's difficult to project his career beyond the type of films he made in the mid-'50s. No one can say where maturity, self-exploration and artistic goals would have taken him. Regarding the image of James Dean, there is no room for this type of speculation. Frozen in time, he is eternally young.

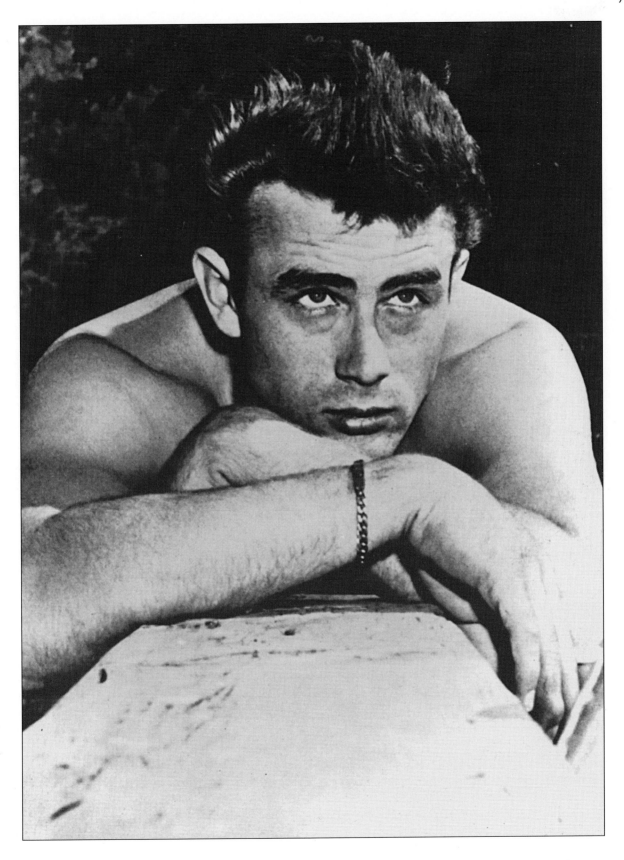

John Derek

Disdainful Youth

John Derek was okay, if you like drop-dead gorgeous. With those Valentino looks, he had a career handed to him on a silver platter and, like the spoiled child at a birthday party, threw it back. John Derek decided he'd rather promote perfect "tens" than be one himself.

This reluctant heartthrob was born Derec Harris in Los Angeles in 1926. Both his parents were in show business. His mother was actress Delores Johnson and his father, writer-director-actor Lawson Harris. While still a teenager, he was put under contract by David O. Selznick. He was unbilled in *Since You Went Away* (1944), then billed as Dare Harris in *I'll Be Seeing You* (1944). After that, he disappeared from films, enlisting in the Army.

When he returned, he was under contract to Twentieth Century Fox for only a year, during which, the story goes, he was uncooperative and unwilling to take direction. He found his way to Columbia Studios, where he was renamed John Derek. Two big "breaks" followed for him: *Knock On Any Door* (1949), which starred Humphrey Bogart and proved a big showcase for young Derek, and *All The King's Men* (1949), in which he portrayed the angry, ill-fated Tom. John Derek was on his way, as Columbia drowned in fan mail for him. Referring to his looks, he told Earl Wilson, "I'm not going to complain . . . it got me a $150 a week contract . . . The ability wasn't there. The looks compensated."

82

All the King's Men. Derek with Broderick Crawford and John Ireland. Columbia, 1949.

Like Tony Curtis and Rock Hudson over at Universal, it was time for Columbia to put Derek through the usual swashbuckling hoops so many young actors were subjected to in the '50s. In short order, he made *Rogues of Sherwood Forest* (1950) and *Mask of the Avenger* (1951), evidently being groomed as an Errol Flynn of sorts. Later, he would make *Prince of Pirates* (1953) and *The Adventures of Hajji Baba* (1954).

"He is a fine man," Tony Curtis said of him, "but he didn't have the intestinal fortitude to want to make it in the movies." It was the money that interested Derek and the money that kept him making films. As he himself is quoted as saying, "I was brought up to think of acting as a girl's profession . . . I was interested in girls, clothes and cars. The only thing the movies ever had for me was money."

Evidently bored beyond belief, he kept grinding out performances, exhibiting a sensual, roguish quality: *Prince of Players* (1955), *The Leather Saint* (1956), Joshua in *The Ten Commandments* (1956), *Omar Khayyam* (1957), *Exodus*

In *Prince of Players* with Richard Burton. 20th Century Fox, 1955.

(1960). But as he told writer Aline Mosby back in 1956, "Why knock yourself out to win Oscars? I want to have fun, without a struggle . . . I want money to spend on my hobbies."

One of his hobbies was photography, which he practiced using his second wife, Ursula Andress, as a subject. After years of wanting to direct, he finally got his chance in *Nightmare in the Sun* (1964) and *Once Before I Die* (1965). In both, he co-starred with Ursula. Neither was particularly well-received by critics.

Having invested his money very well, he was able to quit acting altogether and devote himself to directing, photographing and promoting his various wives, first Ursula, followed by Linda Evans and, finally, Bo Derek. (Derek's first wife was starlet Patti Behrs, by whom he has two children. They were divorced in 1955.) He is known to be difficult on a film set, now that he is behind the scenes.

Today, still very handsome with his mane of white hair, John Derek says of himself, "I have very few friends and almost no acquaintances." Back in 1949, in *Knock on Any Door*, he uttered the classic line, "Live fast, die young and leave a good-looking corpse." He's going for two out of three.

Farley Granger

Working from the Heart

"You astound me — as always," Farley Granger tells John Dall in *Rope*. And likewise, Farley Granger astounds. He is as remarkably handsome as ever, and his resonant, youthful speaking voice remains the same.

James Dean spoke to rebellious youth, Clift to alienated youth. Granger embodied all youth. In films such as *Side Street* (1949), *Edge of Doom* (1950) and the cult classic, *They Live By Night* (1947), he's the basically good kid down on his luck, trying to break free of bad associations. But in the two films he made for Hitchcock, *Rope* (1948) and *Strangers on a Train* (1951), he's affluent youth, the young man with everything, the object of desire, Mr. Preppie.

He was one of the elite from his rather auspicious beginning. At the age of seventeen, he received his first opportunity as one of the principals in *The North Star* (1943) for Samuel Goldwyn. Goldwyn, as Granger tells it, "was one of the early first independents. He did maybe a film a year at most. Unfortunately for me, most of my films had to be on loan-out to MGM, RKO, Fox and Warner. That was very catch-as-catch-can, which I didn't particularly enjoy."

Goldwyn Studios didn't have a young player program, so unlike Tony Curtis, there were no kissing classes for the young man Goldwyn called "Mr. Granger." "They didn't have any of that stuff. Goldwyn was a very independent person.

There was Dana Andrews, Teresa Wright, Danny Kaye, Virginia Mayo — that was about it. He had very few people under contract to him.

"I learned by mistakes. I didn't come up gradually — it might have been better if I had. But I didn't, so that's that. Right away, I was put in a position that I was very young for, and also had no background particularly to cope with it. I was lucky that the first two films I did were with Lewis Milestone, the director. Then I worked with some other good directors who really took care of me, were really very good to me and helped me a great deal. I loved working with Nick Ray [in *They Live by Night*]. I thought he was terrific. And, of course, I enjoyed working with Hitchcock very much. I felt he liked me, and we got along well — I thought that was good, because lots of times, he didn't particularly like actors. He wasn't too kind about them on several occasions.

"But then I began to feel, I really had to do this on my own. I have to know what the heck I'm doing. I can't depend on anybody else."

But Granger did learn about the importance and value of publicity. "They had, as every studio did, their own publicity department, which studios no longer do. Everybody now has to be out on their own. The publicity department just took care of everything whether you wanted them to or not! Nine times out of ten, you'd read something in the paper that was totally bogus,

Warner Brothers publicity still, 1951. Photo credit: Jack Albin.

With Robert Walker in Hitchcock's *Strangers on a Train*. Warner Brothers, 1951.

you know, but the studio had put it out. At first I accepted it, because I didn't know any better. I was very young. And then, after I felt that I was beginning to achieve something, some of it, I thought, was really not proper, and I didn't like it. Many people didn't. A lot of the stories for the movie magazines were completely made up. The articles would say, 'Well, then, Farley said to me . . . and he told me this . . . ,' and I'd never had the interview! It annoyed me, that kind of behavior."

And what about the fans? Like Clift, Granger was serious about his work. How did he feel about young girls being interested in him because of his looks and the types of films he made? "Some of the fans were very, very nice, and some of them were horrendous. I was on a tour where some of the people got hysterical, screamed, yelled, fainted, and the police had to take me out of a Boston theater by the fire escape. I didn't think that was particularly meaningful to what I was trying to do.

"The thing with Clift is that, like Brando, he came from the theater and had a big reputation there. I was a home-grown commodity [born in San Jose,

With James Stewart in Alfred Hitchcock's *Rope*. Warner Brothers, 1958.

California] and found in Hollywood. So I didn't have the advantages that he had as far as experience, so that I could tell them to go to hell. I had to learn the hard way. Hollywood would put up with certain things from Clift. As far as they were concerned, I was being a pain in the neck, because I didn't want to do this or that."

Granger finally bought out his contract from Goldwyn. "He had really no films for me, and I just didn't want to do the loan-out stuff anymore. If they'd pay the price, he would loan me out, whether the film was good or bad." Part of the problem also was, the studios already had actors under contract that, for them, were much cheaper to use. In using Farley Granger, they were increasing him as a commodity — for Goldwyn — and spending more money than was necessary.

"I've always believed — maybe I've done it too much, to a degree — but I always felt I would rather have people saying, 'Where is he? I'd like to see more of him.' Rather than, 'Oh, God, that's him again in some lousy picture. I don't want to see him.' And to do bad work just to work, I don't believe in it, if you don't have to. It's like with television. There's just so much junk. It's good for young people to get experience. But once they have a kind of name, they should be careful."

After leaving Goldwyn, Granger went to Italy and did *Senso* (1954) for Luchino Visconti, an intricate 19th century love story which co-starred Alida Valli. "I enjoyed working with Visconti very much," Farley said. "He was very dictatorial. I had never done any kind of European film before, and I found it absolutely fascinating. I had a six-week contract, and the film went on for six months. I was exhausted from it. Visconti was a true artist in every respect, totally different from the Hollywood people."

After returning to Hollywood for *The Girl in the Red Velvet Swing* (1955), Granger concentrated on television and theater work. "I had great admiration for the theater. When I finally got to New York and saw some theater and met some people involved in it, I developed a great love for the theater. I wanted desperately to work in it. I began more and more to prefer that to film, because I felt you were freer and could do more on stage than in a film. In a film, so much depends on everybody else. That began to work on me."

Granger never abandoned films, but rather than stay in Hollywood, he worked in Europe, in films such as *Qualcosa striscia nel buio* (1970), *Lo chiamavano Trinita* (1971) and *Delitto per Delitto* (1972), among others, enjoying the Italian lifestyle — and character roles — seemingly more than what Hollywood offered.

In the 1948 film, *Rope,* Granger's character, Philip, announces, "They're coming," as he hears the police sirens and knows he will soon be arrested. Quietly, he sits and plays the piano. How unlike Granger's own life or career! He has never waited for anything, and unlike the manipulated Philip, he has taken charge of his own destiny and gone where his heart has led him.

When I asked him if he had any photos he wanted used in the book, he said, "No. Something presentable." He's always been much more than that.

With Alida Valli in Visconti's *Senso* (1954).

ROCK HUDSON

Rock Hudson

Vaulting Ambition

One need only look at the earliest photos of Rock to know what Hollywood saw in him. He gave new definition to the words "handsome" and "masculine." Even though he began in films at the young age of 22, there was no need for him to go through a transition from juvenile to leading man — he was a natural leading man almost from the very beginning. As the last full-fledged movie star to emerge from the studio system, he did much for the stock of Universal, a studio known for its "B" and horror films.

And his stardom meant everything to him.

Roy Scherer, Jr. was born November 17, 1925, in Winnetka, Kansas. Later, he took the name of his stepfather, Fitzgerald. His natural father left the family during the Depression, when he lost his job as an auto mechanic. Rock helped to support his family from the time he was ten. As far as theatrical pursuits, he sang in the high school glee club and church choir. And he managed to see nearly every film that was released and longed to take drama lessons. One of his early idols was actor Jon Hall of *Hurricane* (1937) and *Ali Baba and the Forty Thieves* (1944) fame.

In 1943, he went into the Navy and worked unloading planes from carriers. When the war ground to a halt, he was assigned to laundry detail.

After the Navy, he went to California, where his natural father was living. There, he had a variety of jobs, including that of a truck driver. But ambitious to become an actor, he soon came to the attention of an agent named Henry Willson, who took Rock as a client. The traditional story is that Willson changed the name "Roy Fitzgerald" to "Rock Hudson." But some evidence surfaced later, when Sara Davidson was researching *Rock Hudson: His Story*, that Hudson's name was actually changed by his first agent, Ken Hodge.

After five screen tests and no takers, director Raoul Walsh put him under personal contract, giving the inexperienced newcomer a small part in a film, *Fighter Squadron* (1948). "Pretty soon you're going to have to get a bigger blackboard" was the line he flubbed so many times that it was changed to, "Pretty soon, you'll have to write smaller numbers." The story goes that Walsh didn't cast Hudson again, but did offer him a job painting his house. Walsh sold Hudson's contract to Universal.

There, like Tony Curtis, Jeff Chandler and Piper Laurie, he studied acting with Sophie Rosenstein. Like Curtis, Hudson spoke very highly of the famous drama coach, saying that when he first saw her, he thought she was the ugliest woman he'd ever seen, but after being coached in a role by her, thought she was absolutely beautiful.

Hudson, in later years, would rave about the studio system and the grooming, training and publicity it gave its stars. In his case, it whipped him into shape. What set Hudson apart from a Jeff Chandler or a Tony Curtis, who were ready for more challenging roles, was his lack of acting and technical experience. The early films — *I Was A Shoplifter* (1950), *The Iron Man* (1951), *The Fat Man* (1951), *Here Come the Nelsons* (1952), *The Golden Blade* (1953), *Taza, Son of Cochise* (1954) — helped him learn his craft.

On Hudson's relationship with Universal, Tony Randall, his co-star in the Hudson-Doris Day films, commented, "The studio system made him. It brought him along. He stayed most of his life at Universal. He actually lived on the lot. He had a nice bungalow, and when they were shooting, he wouldn't bother going home. He'd stay there, get up at 5 in the morning, have breakfast with the roundabouts. That was a life. And they treated him right, brought him along slowly. Finally, he began to catch on with the public, and they built him." Randall recalls that at Hudson's peak, he was "the glamour boy of the world. The girls were after him unbelievably. They just swarmed. His dressing room was always full of girls, and the set was always full of girls. He liked having them around."

Over the years, Rock did everything his studio told him to do, in an effort to

In *Peggy*. Universal, 1950.

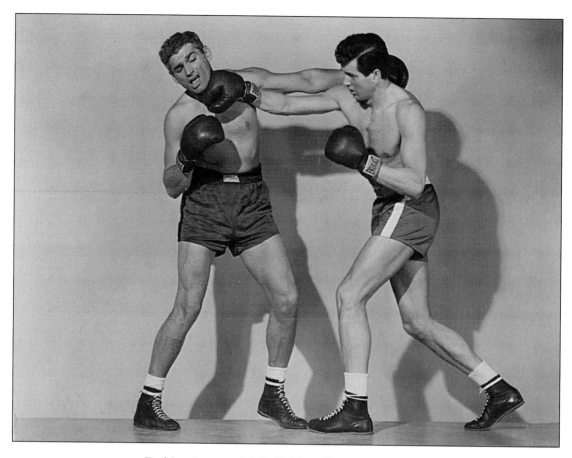

Duking it out with Jeff Chandler in *Iron Man*.
Hudson played Speed and Chandler played Coke. Universal, 1951.

keep what he had, always insecure and afraid of being a nobody again. He did stunt work for no additional pay, assuming it was part of his contractual agreement with the studio. It wasn't. He went on "studio dates" to cover his homosexuality and eventually married his secretary, Phyllis Gates.

All his hard work paid off. By the time *Magnificent Obsession* (1954) rolled around, he was ready. Director Douglas Sirk chose him after Hudson tested with eight scenes. The film that had made Robert Taylor a star in its original version worked the same magic for "Rock Hudson." In 1954, *Modern Screen* named him the most popular actor of the year, and in 1956, he received an Oscar nomination for *Giant*. "So now here's Rock Hudson," said *Look* magazine on March 18, 1958. "He's wholesome . . . His whole appeal is cleanliness and respectability — this boy is pure." Tony Randall said of him, "He was the idealized all-American boy. He really looked like a truck driver who'd gotten some class."

Later, of course, Hudson proved that he had a flair for sophisticated comedy in a series of hit films made with Doris Day: *Pillow Talk* (1959), *Lover Come Back* (1961) and *Send me No Flowers* (1964). About his friend and leading lady in those films, he said they had trouble looking at each other after the first film, because they'd start laughing.

Not much has been written about Rock Hudson's gifts as a story-teller. "He was a funny man," Tony Randall remembers. It is a tragedy that he did not live long enough to write his own book of Hollywood stories. He knew some of the best and funniest of Hollywood anecdotes, and had many amusing experiences he enjoyed relating.

One of Rock's best stories concerned singing "Baby, It's Cold Outside" with Mae West at the 1958 Oscar presentation. Rehearsals with Mae were always an experience — she would keep him waiting and then make a grand entrance. The day of the performance at the Oscars, Rock decided that, rather than go through the front of the theater, he would simply enter through the stage door of the Pantages theater. However, the street leading to the parking lot was roped off.

Back to God's Country. Universal, 1953.

Not recognized by the police, he asked politely if he could be let through, and was told he needed a pass. Going around to another entrance, he obtained a pass and returned to the parking lot, but the policeman, suspicious as to where Rock suddenly found a pass, still would not let him through the barrier. Furious — and now also late — Rock drove down a hill into the parking lot, parked his car, and was storming into the theater, when he was stopped by an attendant who'd seen him drive down the hill. By this time in a cold sweat, Rock said, "Don't mess with me, because I'll kill you," and proceeded into the theater, where he was soundly scolded. "This is television," the staff said to him, "You can't be late like this." Thirty-five years old, a non-singer, and about to sing on live television with a living legend, he was totally traumatized. As he raced onto the stage, he noticed that Mae had positioned the chaise lounge so that he would be reclining behind her, not next to her. In a fit of temper, he grabbed the chaise lounge and threw it down beside her. As he jumped into it, the curtain went up. All the audience saw was Rock singing, suavely, "Baby, It's Cold Outside," with a formidable Mae, who admonished him later — "You mustn't get upset."

After twenty-three years in films, he made a smash in television with "McMillan and Wife." (When the producers wanted to expand the series to two hours, he reportedly said, "Why two hours? The thing doesn't hold up for ninety minutes!") He also performed widely in theater after 1973 in *I Do! I Do!* with Carol Burnett, *Camelot* and *On The Twentieth Century*. Before his failed series, "The Devlin Connection," came along, he was in New York and intending to study acting with the famed teacher Uta Hagen — he had learned long ago the benefits of training. His last film was *The Ambassador* (1986), and his last television appearance was on "Dynasty" in 1985.

This most private and discreet of men died of AIDS on October 2, 1985. When told that there was no longer any way to cover up the fact that he had the dreaded disease, he purportedly said, "Who cares. Go ahead . . . What's the point." Perhaps, after over 30 years in the public eye, he was tired of hiding. "I had one image," he told author Boze Hadleigh, "and the name that promoted it." There was nothing to protect anymore — the beautiful face looked like a skeleton, and he'd made his last public appearance.

Take Care of My Little Girl. 20th Century Fox, 1951.

Jeffrey Hunter

Heaven on the Face

Few actors have come to the movies with Jeffrey Hunter's physical appearance and talent. Even among the best-looking young men in Hollywood, his tall physique, heart-stopping blue eyes and classic features stood out. Early on, he exhibited strong acting ability, intelligence and a willingness to take direction.

Despite all this, Jeffrey Hunter, who originally aspired to be a teacher, was by temperament a most unlikely candidate for stardom, and true stardom, in the end, eluded him. This was due to his tremendous sensitivity, inability to play the Hollywood game, and personal problems that caused him to lose sight of his career goals at a crucial point. The man who played Jesus was, after all, only human.

"Jeffrey Hunter" began life as Henry "Hank" McKinnies, Jr. in New Orleans on November 25, 1926. His parents moved to Whitefish Bay, Wisconsin when Hank was 5. There, he grew up as an only child, excelling in athletics and scholastic achievement.

He enlisted in the Navy when war came. After naval service, Hunter attended Northwestern University and UCLA, majoring at the latter in speech and radio. But he never received his Master's degree — talent scouts from Paramount in the audience of a student production whisked him away before graduation.

108

With Natalie Wood in *The Searchers*. Warner Brothers, 1956. Photo credit: Alexander Kahle.

With a script girl on the set of *Sailor of the King*. 20th Century Fox, 1951.

Although Paramount was going through upheaval at that time and did not sign young Hank, Twentieth Century Fox did. Fox changed his name to Jeffrey Hunter, and he joined Dale Robertson, Robert Wagner, Debra Paget and Jean Peters as "up-and-comings" there. In his first film, *Fourteen Hours* (1951), he played Debra Paget's love interest and, as he said later, had more lines to say than Grace Kelly, who also made her debut in that film.

After *Fourteen Hours*, Hunter was shuttled from film to film. Most notable in those early years were: *Lure of the Wilderness* (a remake of *Swamp Water*), in which he co-starred with Jean Peters in 1952, *Red Skies of Montana* (1952) and a British film, *Sailor of the King* (1953). He quickly became very popular with teens — especially after they saw those blue eyes in color in *Red Skies of Montana*. He began to receive enormous amounts of fan mail.

But it didn't last long. Robert Wagner quickly became the Juvenile Prince of Fox (literally as well as figuratively, when he won the role of Prince Valiant). Hunter found himself often playing a supporting role to Wagner's lead. He realized, finally, that he wasn't in Whitefish Bay anymore — nothing was going to be handed to him. Frustrated and unhappy, he asked Fox to release him from his contract. The brass discouraged him from this, with promises of better things. These better things did appear, not at Fox, but in the form of loan-outs.

Young Jeffrey Hunter's career changed dramatically when he fought for, and won, the role of Martin Pawley in *The Searchers* (1956). *The Searchers* today is considered a classic film, with directors such as Spielberg and Scorcese claiming inspiration from it. Directed by the great John Ford, it starred John Wayne, along with Hunter and Natalie Wood. "I was told I had really arrived," Hunter said, "because they gave me almost as much ammunition as they gave John Wayne." But Jeffrey Hunter almost wasn't a part of the film. Ford told him, "You're not the type" to play the part-Indian Martin. The actor made himself up in darker pancake, slicked down his hair and went back to Ford, who let him test for the role.

Hunter received wonderful reviews as Wayne's sidekick. The *New York Herald Tribune* said, "Jeffrey Hunter is excellent as the boy who shares his [Wayne's] relentless search. He is far more emotional and likable, and he matures over the five years from a naive kid to a man who can take care of himself in tough situations."

"I have a certain value now as a teenage commodity," Jeffrey Hunter once said to a reporter, "but who knows how long this will last?" The time had come to move into more mature roles. John Ford used him twice more, for *The Last Hurrah* (1958) and *Sergeant Rutledge* (1960). "*Sergeant Rutledge* may not be John Ford's masterpiece," Paul Beckley of the *Herald Tribune* wrote, "but it is a sweet breeze . . . Jeffrey Hunter turns in, under Ford's influence, the best performance of his young career." He played an espionage agent in a British independent, *Count Five and Die* (1957), a Korean war vet in *No Down Payment* (1957), and a tough marine in *In Love and War* (1958). Of the successful *Hell To Eternity* (1960), the true story of marine Guy Gabaldon, Howard Thompson of *The New York Times* said, "Mr. Hunter finally comes into his own with the best acting of his career."

Then, another turn in Jeffrey Hunter's career — *King of Kings* (1961). According to *King*'s director, Nicholas Ray, Hunter's mesmerizing blue eyes and personal charisma, noted while Ray worked with him on *The True Story of Jesse James* (1957), won him the role of Christ. During the filming in Spain, Hunter was often mistaken for Christ by peasants. After the film was released, his fan mail not only increased, but he received letters from people asking for solutions to their problems. It was a heavy load to carry, and he didn't bear up well under

Hunter and Joanne Woodward in a publicity pose for *A Kiss Before Dying*.
United Artists, 1956.

As Jesus in *King of Kings*. MGM, 1961.

it, especially with the joke that circulated Hollywood that the film had been renamed *I Was a Teenage Jesus.*

Evaluating the importance of this role in Hunter's career is a difficult one, as is assessing his performance. Career-wise, playing Jesus was not an inspired choice; however, *King of Kings* is the film for which he is most remembered today, and is the reason that, long after his death, the Jeffrey Hunter Fan Club continued to exist.

As far as the film itself, a problem with the sound track meant that Hunter had to re-record his role in a sound studio. This was extremely unfortunate. His speech training had given him a beautiful speaking voice — he had experience as a radio actor — but his voice is not used to its best effect in *King of Kings.* Although reviews of his portrayal were mixed or downright cruel at the time, the film, and Hunter's performance, hold up very well today.

The demise of Jeff Hunter's career has often been laid at the feet of Jesus. This, strictly speaking, isn't true. He was not typecast, nor was he ever at a loss for acting work. Had he reassessed his career and obtained good advice, he could have continued to grow as an actor. But the role had scared him. The criticism had stung, and due to strong personal loyalties that kept him from seeking top-notch advisors, he basically fell off the career track, despite some good parts — as a hen-pecked thief in *Man-Trap* (1961), *No Man Is An Island* (1962), a true World War II story, and *The Longest Day* (1962).

Hunter's best friend and college roommate, writer/director Lee Riordan, said that in the early '60s, Hunter "admitted he was disappointed with how things were going. He thought his career would have been stronger by that time. He wouldn't listen to negative things about certain people around him."

Hunter eventually found a good deal of work on television, and then in Europe. Interestingly, on television, he often played not heroes, but psychotics, indicating he could quite possibly have had a "second career" in character roles. His incredible good looks had kept him from this type of role early in his career. "This face of mine," he said to a reporter in 1965, "Shouldn't the ravages of time be doing something to it?"

Now sometimes billed as "Jeff Hunter," he was hired in 1965 by Gene Roddenberry to play the lead in a pilot, "Star Trek: The Cage." But when NBC ordered a second pilot, Hunter was not available. The rest is history — for the "Star Trek" actors. For Hunter, it was on to another bad film. Marital problems and the ensuing financial responsibilities of alimony and child support pressured him to keep working.

The latter part of his film career is peppered with roles in sub-B films, often made in Spain, such as *Witch Without a Broom* (1966), *The Christmas Kid* (1968) and *Sexy Susan Sins Again* (1969). However, around the time of his death, it looked as if Hunter was gently but firmly re-establishing himself in the mainstream, with roles in *Guide for the Married Man* (1967), *The Private Navy of Sergeant O'Farrell* (1968) and some good television roles.

On May 26, 1969, Jeffrey Hunter was found unconscious at the bottom of some stairs in his home, where he lived with his third wife. The police surmised that he tripped over a planter and had been knocked unconscious. He died the next morning, after brain surgery. An autopsy revealed he had suffered a stroke, then fallen. The actor had been suffering dizzy spells, probably from cerebral bleeding, the result of an explosion on a film set in Spain. At the time of his death, he was 42.

Lee Riordan said of Hunter, "He was the finest, most decent man I've ever known." It may not be a Hollywood tribute, but it's sure not a bad way to be remembered.

Gold for the Caesars. MGM, 1964.

Tab Hunter

An Unquestionable Spirit

Few actors have enjoyed the variety in their careers that Tab Hunter has. How many actors can say they've played opposite everyone from Rita Hayworth to Divine?

Nowadays, with the likes of Robert Redford and Harrison Ford, the fair leading man is more commonplace. But in the '50s, Tab Hunter stood as the lone blond. It was a gamble that paid dividends for Warner Brothers — only Rock Hudson and Tony Curtis matched him in popularity. In 1958, in a poll of twenty-year old women, Tab Hunter and President Eisenhower tied for fourth place as ideal husband material.

Tab Hunter was born Arthur Gelien on July 11, 1931, in New York City. When he was two, the family moved to San Francisco. At the age of fifteen and a half, he lied about his age and joined the Coast Guard. While in service school in New York, he saw Broadway shows and caught the acting bug.

Once out of the service, he concentrated on ice skating, winning the California junior pair championship in 1949 and the California senior pair championship in 1950. He continued ice skating even during his busy acting career — he was unable to do a figure skating competition in Lake Placid due to a commitment to the film, *Sea Chase* (1955).

In 1949, a friend, Dick Clayton, a former juvenile leading man who later became Burt Reynolds' agent, got him a bit part in *The Lawless*. Tab Hunter had one line — "Hi, Fred" — which was cut. Clayton is credited with creating the name "Tab Hunter." Supposedly, the conversation went something like, "We have to tab him something. He likes to ride hunters and jumpers. Why not Tab Hunter?"

Hunter's opinion of this was expressed to writer David Galligan some years later: "I was what they called 'a product' of Hollywood. That's the worst label you can put on somebody, and then to hang a name like 'Tab' on top of that is pretty bad."

Hunter's athletic physique and brilliant looks brought him to the attention of director Stuart Heisler, who signed him for the lead in *Island of Desire* (1952). As Hunter told reporter Sidney Skolsky, "It was more important to look good almost nude than to be an actor." Hunter was dubbed "The Sigh Guy," and the sighs from teenagers were heard in Hollywood.

Hunter cashed in on being a dreamboat, but he was no fool. He knew if he didn't overcome a vapid, pretty-boy image, his career would be short-lived.

Out on the town with Natalie Wood and Tony Perkins, 1956.

Tab Hunter and Mona Freeman in *Battle Cry*. Warner Brothers, 1955.

Having come into the business with no background as an actor, he made attempts to change that, working with drama teacher Jeff Corey privately, too shy to work in a classroom situation. He also took voice lessons, and in 1957, hit it big with "Young Love," which sold 1,300,000 records within two months of its release.

Hunter also sought out good directors, working with both George Stevens and Luchino Visconti in screen tests only, but taking the opportunity to learn what he could. When James Dean was working on *Rebel Without a Cause*, Hunter stepped in and helped test Carroll Baker for *Giant*. Although he lost the lead in Luchino Visconti's *Senso* to Farley Granger (Hunter's agent said, "Luchino who?"), he did all the tests with Claudia Cardinale for another Visconti film, *Rocco and His Brothers* (1960). Columbia, a prime investor, nixed him for the role in that movie, calling him "not hot."

Despite these disappointments, his hard work yielded benefits. He made some very good films: *Track of the Cat* (1954), *Battle Cry* (1955), *The Burning Hills*

(1956), *Damn Yankees* (1958), *They Came to Cordura* (1959) and *The Pleasure of His Company* (1961). *The Burning Hills*, based on a Louis L'Amour novel, sported a young cast — Hunter, Natalie Wood, Skip Homeier and Earl Holliman — and Bosley Crowther of *The New York Times* wrote of it, "Tab Hunter and Natalie Wood, a couple of youngsters who seem to be winning popularity with teen-agers . . . come out all right and are now in the club." He then added ". . . the principal players . . . look very nice all mussed up."

As Hunter once said, "The three most important things in this business are material, material, material." And he sought out good material wherever he could. "Playhouse 90" afforded him some of his best: "Forbidden Area," in which he played a Russian spy, and "Portrait of a Murderer" with Geraldine Page. It was Page that Tab Hunter credits with some great advice: "If they don't like you, that's their bad taste." He also proved he couldn't be pushed around, taking a suspension rather than work on a film he didn't like, *Darby's Rangers* (1958).

When the newer blonds — i.e., Troy Donahue — came in, Tab Hunter found his reign over. As he himself put it, "How long could I go on saying things like 'Dad, can I have the keys to the big car tonight?'" He summed up his philosophy to writer Lewis Archibald this way in 1982: "In Hollywood, you can go to bed one night and wake up the next morning, and you're 65 years old and you haven't done a damn thing . . . I think no matter what you do in life, you have to be a doer." Hunter decided if there wasn't anything for him in Hollywood anymore, he would go where there was something.

Like many cast-off dreamboats, Hunter headed for Europe and made spaghetti westerns, refusing, in some cases, to walk on the set without his salary in hand — it was that kind of atmosphere. Back in this country, he made *The Life and Times of Judge Roy Bean* (1972), did some television, and found steady work in dinner theater, in plays like *Chapter Two, 6 Rms, Riv Vu, The Tender Trap* and *Here Lies Jeremy Troy*. Audiences were glad to see him, and he proved a big draw.

While working in Indianapolis, he received the offer to play Divine's love interest in *Polyester*. No longer having a film agent, Hunter closed the deal himself. As drive-in owner Todd Tomorrow, the love interest of the 300-pound transvestite Divine ("She has more on the ball than any other leading lady I've ever worked with"), Hunter made his film comeback. *Grease II* and *Lust in the Dust* (1985) followed.

"I'm either an old new face or a new old face," he says. Hollywood chewed him up and spit him out, but Tab Hunter has survived in his own way, pursuing

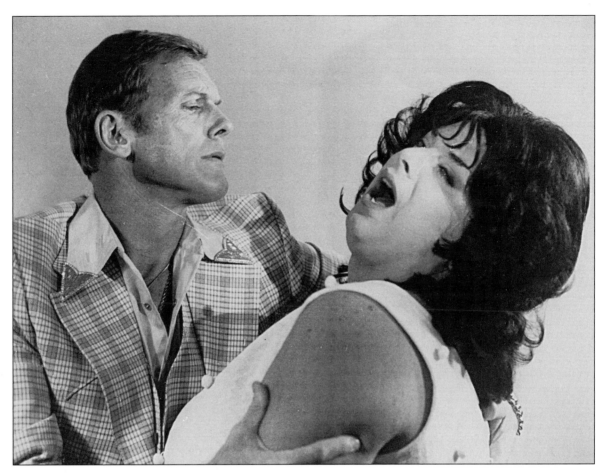

With Divine (Glenn Milstead) in *Polyester*. New Line Cinema, 1981.

not only acting, but horse training. Although he has suffered ill health (a heart attack and a stroke) in the past few years, Tab Hunter can still smile at himself. Perhaps his most prototypical quote is one he gave at the time of *Polyester*'s release: "Divine and I could end up being the William Powell and Myrna Loy of the '80s." And in that kind of attitude lies the key to his survival.

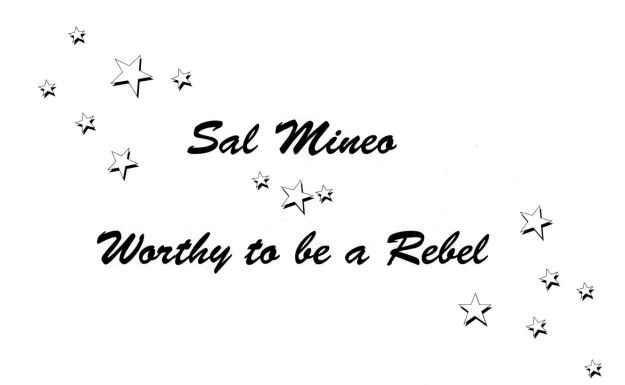

Sal Mineo
Worthy to be a Rebel

Hollywood called him "The Switchblade Kid," and as he died by the switchblade, the title proved prophetic. By the time he was murdered at age 36, Sal Mineo had experienced all the ups and downs of Hollywood — from 10,000 fan letters a week and two Oscar nominations, to the inability to get a role. It was tough going for the man who had once been dubbed "King of the '50s."

Sal wasn't one to mince words, as an interview he gave to writer Boze Hadleigh in *Conversations with My Elders* testifies, in which he called Paul Newman "a walking ice cube" and Jeffrey Hunter "a creep." His actions were as direct as his conversation. He was one of the few stars who bucked the studio by refusing to change his name or mask his sexual preference by marrying. Mineo never did much to hide his homosexual leanings. He stated he'd had an affair with Peter Lawford, a remark printed in the *New York Post*, the newspaper which also revealed that Mineo and Rock Hudson dated.

This little Italian-American dynamo, born in 1939 in the Bronx, where his father had a casket-making firm, came to Hollywood from Broadway, where he played in *The Rose Tattoo* and then, at the age of eleven, the Crown Prince in *The King and I*. He made his film debut in *Six Bridges to Cross* (1955), and then catapulted to teen idol status in *Rebel Without a Cause* (1955). "Come on," his character, Plato, pleads with James Dean, as he attempts to join his gang, "I ain't no kid — I can take care of myself." Mineo spoke to every teen who wanted to fit in, to be one of the crowd. This film brought him his first Oscar nomination.

With those major bedroom eyes and his trademark leather jacket, Sal exuded a wiry energy, a sensitivity and a feistiness that appealed to teens. Throughout the '50s, his popularity was tremendous and extended into the music world, where he enjoyed a career as a singer. "Sal Sings," released by Epic Records in 1958, was a compilation of his hits. He made very youth-oriented films like *Rock, Pretty Baby* (1956) and *Dino* (1957). "I think," he told *TV Guide* in 1957, trying to explain the furor, "they [teens] idolize actors who are on their side . . . Kids get pushed around a lot . . . When they find somebody who they think understands their problems, they make him a hero." In 1956, he played a juvenile delinquent in *Crime in the Streets*. When it opened in a theater on Broadway, Mineo was there to sign autographs. The pandemonium from the crush of fans was so great that he had to be removed from the theater by the police.

"TNT — The Teens' New Thrill, a bundle of Dynamite," *Photoplay* magazine hailed him in 1958. "HE LOVES," one column was headed, listing his boxer, Bimbo, and his mother's cooking. "HE DISLIKES" — spinach and girls who

Rebel Without a Cause: Sal Mineo, James Dean, Natalie Wood. Warner Brothers, 1955.

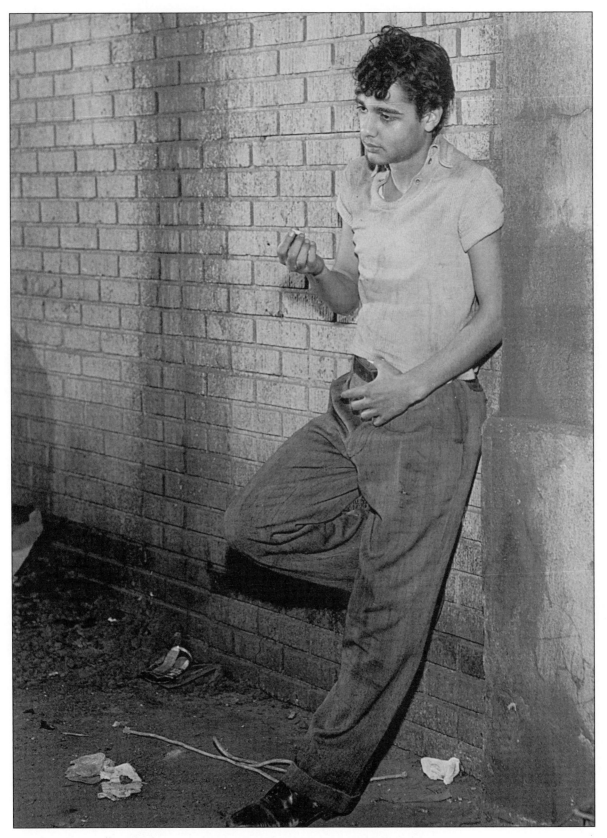

Somebody Up There Likes Me. MGM, 1956.

Exodus, with Jill Haworth. United Artists, 1960.

telephone him. "HE FEELS" — protective of his sister and pride for his older brothers. "HE THINKS" — teens should be treated as individuals. "HE DATES" — girls with a lot of personality. "HE WANTS" — to please his fans.

Teen idols, like child stars, have an important transition to make. Sal was both a teen idol and a child star, and found a transition to adult stardom out of his grasp well into his twenties. Further complicating things was his ethnic appearance — not a detriment in today's Hollywood, but certainly one in the '50s. After roles in films like *Somebody Up There Likes Me* (1957), *Tonka* (1958, as an Indian), *Exodus* (1960, for which he received his second Oscar nomination), *Cheyenne Autumn* (1964) and *The Greatest Story Ever Told* (1965) ("I ought to see it again some time, for laughs," he told Boze Hadleigh), Sal found acting roles harder and harder to get. He was interested in buying the rights to the novel, *Midnight Cowboy*, but nothing materialized. His last film was *Escape from Planet of the Apes* (1971), five years before his murder.

"It would be easy," he told writer Stephen Lewis, "to blame Hollywood, to say that I was typed and forced to play the same role over and over. For a while, I did. But the truth is that I knew what I was doing. I was enjoying myself."

Returning to the stage brought him an artistic satisfaction he never found in film, and enabled him to be more open about his sexuality. In 1969, he directed, and then replaced the ailing star, in *Fortune and Men's Eyes*, a play about prison homosexuality, which co-starred Don Johnson. An exacting taskmaster, Mineo conducted rehearsals in actual prisons to give his actors a sense of reality. "An actor," he was quoted as saying, "creates a character, sure, but a director is far more creative. He's the one who really brings a story to life." Although he was praised for his own performance in the role of Rocky, Mineo felt he was too old for the part, and that in the role, which was like many he played in film, he was too familiar to the audience.

His closeness to James Dean was demonstrated in the program for *Fortune* — one page contained a photo of Dean with the inscription, "Jimmy: In memory of your friendship and inspiration, I dedicate this production to you. Sal." Mineo felt he learned self-esteem and pride in his own individuality from Dean. However, he refused to discuss the depth of his relationship with Dean (rumored to be an affair), telling Boze Hadleigh his memories were too personal.

1976 found Mineo considering an offer to pose for *Playgirl* magazine and rehearsing his role as a bisexual cat burglar in *P.S. Your Cat is Dead*. Returning to his West Hollywood apartment building one night after rehearsal, he was knifed while in the carport. (Mineo owned the building with attorney Marvin Mitchelson.) At the time of Sal's death, there was wide speculation that the murderer was an ex-lover or a male prostitute. The real truth, on the other hand, received virtually no coverage in the press. His murderer was a robber, who, while serving time at Jackson State Prison in Michigan, found out that the man he killed — at random — was Sal Mineo.

Mineo was asked by Stephen Lewis in 1969 if he had ever felt any responsibility to the teenagers he represented — after all, he was their idol. "It was groovy," he said. "It was a new thing for kids to know that they had a voice . . . I wasn't trying to build an image. I was trying to build a life for myself."

A Private's Affair. 20th Century Fox, 1959.

Dale Robertson

The Natural Touch

Unlike Robert Wagner, Dale Robertson has aged through the years. His hair is white, his voice gravelly, and his body has lost some of its former athletic look. He embodies, as he always has, the tough westerner, although now it's usually the irascible tough westerner. Back in the '50s, playing opposite Betty Grable, Linda Darnell, Mitzi Gaynor and Jeanne Crain, he was hot stuff and, as everything from fan magazines to the novel, *The Thorn Birds,* will tell you, a major dreamboat.

Dale Robertson was born Dayle Lymoine Robertson in Harrah, Oklahoma. He removed the "y" himself early in life. When he was just a teenager, Will Rogers, a friend of his family's, wanted to take him to Hollywood, but Mrs. Robertson wanted Dale to have an education instead. Rogers advised her not to give Dale drama lessons, saying, "The drama coaches will put your voice in dinner jackets, and most people like their grits and hominy in everyday clothes." Probably for that reason, Robertson never succumbed to speech lessons to remove his "good ol' boy" accent.

After winning twenty-eight letters in sports at Oklahoma Military, he entered military service in 1942 as a private and achieved the rank of first lieutenant, attached to General George Patton's Third Army. Toward the end of the war, he was shot in the knee. It took two operations and nine months for him to recover.

With Charles Korvin in *Lydia Bailey*. 20th Century Fox, 1952.

The shattered knee destroyed his chances for a promising boxing career. He left the service in 1946, having won the Cross of Lorraine, the Silver Star, the Bronze Star and the Purple Heart.

While still in the service and stationed in San Luis Obispo, Robertson went to a Hollywood photographer to have his photo taken for his mother. The photographer, Marion Parsons, blew up the photo and displayed it in her studio window. She later contacted Robertson, explaining that movie agents wanted to talk to him, and offers of screen tests followed. "Most of the leading men were in the service," Robertson said, "and Hollywood was ready to settle for anyone."

By the time he was discharged, the situation had changed mightily. He could not find a job in his native Oklahoma, and Hollywood, bombarded with handsome leading men, was no longer interested. But he decided to persevere in Hollywood, going on agent interviews and working as a clothes model. He studied film editing, stage design and writing at the University of California, but not acting, keeping in mind the advice of Will Rogers.

On the set of *The Silver Whip* with Lola Albright. 20th Century Fox, 1953.

After signing with agents Ned Marin and Charles Feldman, he was taken on the studio rounds, and Twentieth-Century Fox ordered a test. Robertson said of it, "I was bad." Through his agent's brother, he was cast to play Jesse James in a Randolph Scott film, *Fighting Men of the Plains* (1949), a Nat Holt Production. When the film was previewed at a Long Beach theater, the audience went wild for Robertson, and he was mauled when he left the theater. A studio executive said, "It was valid. No young man could have that many relatives." When the film was released, Robertson was called the "m-mm" (mass magnetism) hero.

Darryl F. Zanuck ordered another test, and in 1949, Robertson was given a seven-year contract. "I figure 20th Century Fox signed me for what I was, the way I talk and all," he once said, "and I'm not reckoning to put my words in any dinner jackets."

A role in *Two Flags West* (1950) followed, then larger roles in *Call Me Mister* (1951) and *Take Care of My Little Girl* (1951). During this time, Robertson gained additional experience by spending time on the Fox sound stages, offering to test with actresses under consideration for roles. In 1952, he was cast as the lead in the big-budget *Lydia Bailey*. The film had been turned down by Tyrone Power. "He's an illustrator's dream," Hedda Hopper sighed in 1951, "over six feet of all-American he-man with the Oklahoman's easy approach."

His rugged looks and macho toughness, plus his somewhat limited range, landed him in numerous westerns: *Sitting Bull* (1954), *A Day of Fury* (1956), *Dakota Incident* (1956), ad infinitum. All in all, he made sixty-two films.

Robertson found his way into television and had great success in his series, "The Tales of Wells Fargo," in the late '50s and early '60s. Other series followed: "Iron Horse" in 1966 and "J.J. Starbuck" in 1987.

In 1974, he recorded his first country-western album. Through the years, he has developed a quarter-horse breeding business with his brother, Chet, in his beloved Oklahoma. He told reporter Kathryn Baker in 1987, "I'll never retire till they plant me, you know . . . not from the horse business, the oil business, the picture business, none of them."

Robert Wagner

Gallant Youth

"There are few things as important in this business as timing," Robert Wagner is fond of saying. He should know. No one's timing has ever been better.

This most durable of stars was born February 10, 1930, in Detroit. His well-to-do family moved to Los Angeles when he was nine, and as he once told writer Edith Efron, "I used to try to jump over the wall of the Fox studios and watch 'em make pictures." As a caddy at the Bel-Air Country Club, he met the likes of Clark Gable, Fred Astaire and Alan Ladd, who gave him tips on acting and breaking into the movies.

He also polished airplanes at Clover Field. One day, after polishing Brian Donlevy's plane at Clover Field, Donlevy gave Wagner a five-dollar tip and suggested that he buy a book on dramatics. "I did," he told Sidney Skolsky in 1952, "but learning to act from a book was like learning to ride without a horse."

In short order, his valuable Hollywood connections led him to be discovered by the agent of dreamboats, Henry Willson. Wagner was an extra and did bits for many of the studios, until Willson brought him to Fox, where they gave him what was called a ninety-day test option. Wagner prepared for the test, but also tested at MGM for a film called *Teresa* (1951). This was against studio policy in

With Susan Hayward in *With a Song in My Heart*. 20th Century Fox, 1952.

On the set of *Prince Valiant* with Janet Leigh. 20th Century Fox, 1954.

those days. Before MGM cast John Ericson in the role Wagner tested for, a columnist reported that Wagner, a "dark horse," was heavily in the running for the lead in *Teresa*. As a result, Fox pushed his test through in four days instead of ninety. In a month, he had a big role in *The Halls of Montezuma* (1950), followed by *Let's Make it Legal* (1951). Nothing happened.

Then Susan Hayward was signed to make *With a Song In My Heart* (1952), and Fox assigned Wagner a small part. As Wagner told reporter Mike Connelly, "It was the right time and the right break. The first week the picture was in release, I got 12,000 fan letters. I was on my way."

Well, that turned out to be true as far as Fox was concerned, but not as far as Wagner was concerned. Wagner told the *New York World Telegram and Sun* that the head of the studio, Darryl F. Zanuck, "brought me on as a sort of Tyrone Power. But he [Zanuck] resigned, and I was left there with a tennis racket in one hand and a beach ball in the other." Wagner felt the studio was bound and determined to keep him a juvenile. They also constantly reminded him he could be replaced, by having young actors who resembled him appear on the set.

Wagner and Jeffrey Hunter were the young princes of the Fox lot in the early '50s and, at first, seemingly viewed as interchangeable by the studio. They both took similar juvenile roles in big-budget films: Wagner in *Titanic* (1953) and *Broken Lance* (1954), Hunter in *Red Skies of Montana* (1952) and *Dreamboat* (1952), among the many films they both did.

But the two actors also worked a great deal together, and as the years progressed, the studio showed its opinion of Wagner as the more important star: *White Feather* (1955) (Wagner was the hero, Hunter was an Indian), *The True Story of Jesse James* (1957) (Wagner was Jesse, Hunter was Frank James). In the end, however, neither were really to be well-served by Fox's intention to make them perennial juveniles.

1954 proved pivotal for Wagner. There was *Prince Valiant*. ("I looked like Jane Wyman in that wig.") His notices were mixed. But that same year, he did *Broken Lance* with Spencer Tracy, who liked him and requested him for *The Mountain* (1956). Wagner's acting stock rose still further with *The Hunters* (1957), as he began to make that critical transition from juvenile to leading man. One of the reviews said, "Robert Wagner never had it so good! He gives a glib, flip performance as a brash, brave, be-bop talking pilot which, at last, stamps him as a player of distinction." This led to a showy role in *In Love and War* (1958, which also starred Jeffrey Hunter) for Jerry Wald.

Wagner, Terry Moore and cast on the set of *Beneath the 12 Mile Reef*. 20th Century Fox, 1953.

A Kiss Before Dying with Joanne Woodward. United Artists, 1956.

With wife Natalie Wood, 1959.

Fox, determined to keep his appeal geared to the younger set, wanted him to do a picture with Elvis. He ended his association with the studio in the early '60s, and by the late '60s had found massive success in television as a debonair leading man: "It Takes a Thief," "Switch," "Hart to Hart" and "Lime Street." His sharp business sense, good taste in scripts and great charm have helped him vault over his competition, until now, he is in a class by himself.

His popularity today is as undiminished as his handsome looks. Wagner seems to have weathered it all, from teen-idol stardom and the rigors of television, to his wife, Natalie Wood's, death by drowning in 1981 and the ensuing speculation about the circumstances of her death. "When I was first under contract," he told an interviewer, "I was one of 150 kids. None of the others got anywhere." Robert Wagner made sure he would never be one of the crowd.

John Ericson

The charming, German-born leading man (real name Joseph Meibes) made his film debut in *Teresa* (1951). Shortly thereafter, he won the New York Critics' Award as the stage's most promising newcomer for his performance on Broadway in *Stalag 17*. Although he was advised that MGM was letting actors go, not signing them, Ericson went to Dore Schary, reminded him of his good work in *Teresa*, and asked to be tested for *Rhapsody*. He beat the odds and won a contract at MGM. Today, he remembers how excited he was at the prospect of being able to go on location. "I always loved that about the movies: new places, new people." He co-starred with Vittorio Gassman and Elizabeth Taylor in *Rhapsody* (1954), then appeared in *Green Fire* (1954), *Bad Day at Black Rock* (1954), *The Student Prince* (1954), and others.

As per MGM's promise of "We'll do right by you," Ericson, an excellent actor with discerning taste, was able to turn down films he didn't want, and after two years, asked to be released from his contract. In the '60s and '70s, he did *Pretty Boy Floyd* (1960), *The Seven Faces of Dr. Lao* (1964), *The Money Jungle* (1968), *Bedknobs and Broomsticks* (1971), and began to work a great deal in Europe.

What John Ericson remembers most about MGM was the "warm, charming

John Ericson and Elizabeth Taylor in *Rhapsody.* MGM, 1954.

and caring people. It was like a family." He said that in television, the producer would come to the set the first day and welcome the actors. He laments that Hollywood is not that way today. But, as Ericson put it, although he chooses not to be as active, he's "still working at it" (his resume lists numerous television and regional theater appearances), has an excellent agent, and is writing screenplays with his wife, actress Karen Ericson. He is also an accomplished artist, and his work was recently featured in a one-man show, as well as appearing in a new book, *Actors as Artists.* When I thanked him for calling me, he said, "You wrote such a nice letter, it would have been rude of me not to respond."

A rare man, for sure.

Robert Francis

Handsome, muscular and blond Robert Francis' career was cut short by a fatal plane crash in 1955, when he was 25 years old. He made his film debut as Ensign Willie Keith in *The Caine Mutiny* (1954), and went on to appear in *They Rode West* (1954), *Bamboo Prison* (1954) and *The Long Gray Line* (1955), playing important roles in all. Talking about his career, he once said, "I can always go back to running a ski shop. How many winters can there be without snow?"

George Nader

This handsome, well-built Universal graduate made his debut in *Monsoon* in 1952. His film career never really caught fire — other credits include *Carnival Story* (1954), *The Second Greatest Sex* (1955) and *Away All Boats* (1956). One theory for his not making it into the mainstream is that Universal gave *Confidential* a story on Nader's sex life, so the magazine wouldn't print a story about Rock Hudson's homosexuality. (See the chapter on Rory Calhoun.) Maybe. It seems unlikely, however. Nader

probably just wasn't superstar material. He had three television series, "Ellery Queen" (1956), "The Man and the Challenge" (1959) and "Shannon" (1961), before heading for Europe, where he became known in films as a James Bond type. His novel, *Chrome*, was published in 1978.

George Nader and Jane Powell in *The Female Animal*. Universal, 1958.

Jeff Richards

Jeff Richards had "dreamboat" written all over him, but after a promising start with MGM in *Seven Brides for Seven Brothers* (1954) and *The Opposite Sex* (1956), his career fizzled. I personally think this is a tragedy, having fallen in love with him when he did his TV series, "Jefferson Drum," in the late '50s . Other films include: *Angels in the Outfield* (1951), *The Marauders* (1955) and *Don't Go Near the Water* (1957). Although writer David Ragan lists Richards as having died in 1989, this seems in error. His friends are sworn to secrecy about what he's doing today (but I was permitted to have a letter forwarded to him). He was rumored to be working construction on the Paramount lot in the '70s. One of his friends told me that Jeff Richards is in hiding. He didn't say from what.

Photo Credits:

Kobal Collection: Front cover, pp. 6, 7, 9, 12, 13, 15, 16, 25, 28, 29, 31, 32, 40, 42, 48, 54, 62, 63, 67, 68, 72, 74, 79, 80, 82, 83, 84, 85, 86, 88, 89, 90, 93, 104, 108, 111, 116, 119, 122, 124, 126, 128, 130, 132, 140, 143, 144, 145, 149, 150 bottom.

Photofest: pp. 4, 8, 10, 14, 18, 19, 20, 22, 24, 26, 35, 36, 38, 44, 45, 46, 49, 50, 53, 57, 58, 60, 64, 70, 76, 77, 78, 94, 96, 99, 100, 101, 102, 106, 109, 112, 118, 121, 123, 127, 134, 135, 137, 138, 141, 142, 146, 148, 150 top, 151.

Globe Photos: p. 55

Wehrlundpük Archivalien: pp. 2, 115

Jack Larson: p. 5

Sharon Good: Back cover